MW00488380

CONFESSING
God's Word

Dr. Maureen Anderson

Winword
publishing house

Phoenix, Arizona

SECOND EDITION - 3RD PRINTING

Published by **Winword Publishing, Inc.**
3520 East Brown Road, Mesa, Arizona 85213

ISBN   978-1-58588-131-4 hardcover
        978-1-58588-150-5 softcover/paperback
        978-1-58588-155-0 leather cover

Confessing God's Word

To order or for more information, contact us at:
480-985-6156
or visit: www.maureenanderson.org

Bible versions that are abbreviated within the text:

AMP	Amplified Bible
BE	Basic English Bible
GN	Good News Bible
LB	Living Bible
KJV	King James Version
ML	Modern Language
NASNT	New American Standard NT
NB	New Berkeley
NEB	New English Bible
NIV	New International Version
NKJV	New King James Version
PE	Plain English
SG	Smith - Goodspeed
TNT	Translator's NT
20th C	20th Century
WEY	Weymouth

TABLE OF CONTENTS

Introduction

It is impossible to underestimate how important the Word of God is in our lives. There are so many facets to the Word that we have only begun to understand what it means to embrace it. It brings us life, as Deuteronomy 8:3 tells us. It discerns the thoughts and intentions of the heart, as Hebrews 4:12 says. Existence itself is upheld by God's Word, as Hebrews 1:3 tell us. It changes us, and it changes circumstances. We cannot be successful in life without it.

How do we incorporate the promises and the power of the Word

CONFESSING *God's Word*

into our lives? That is the reason for this book. *Confessing God's Word* is designed to help you tap into the Word of God more effectively and more consistently. There are basically three things that we need to do for the Word to really impact our lives. We need to hear the word over and over, we need to meditate on it and we need to speak the Word or confess it.

One of the most important things that we gain from the Word is faith. This is important, since Hebrews 11:6 says that without faith it is impossible to please God. How do we get faith from the Word? By hearing it.

INTRODUCTION

So then faith comes by hearing,
and hearing by the word of God.
(Romans 10:17 NKJV)

In the original Greek, this means
more than just hearing it once and
not thinking about it again. It
literally refers to hearing the Word
again and again and again. It is
important to constantly fill ourselves
with the Word. We cannot hear it
enough.

Secondly, we need to meditate on
the Word. We must let it sink into
the deepest part of our thinking so
that everything we think is in line
with the Word. This is what God
told Joshua was necessary for him
to succeed.

CONFESSING *God's Word*

This Book of the Law shall not depart from your mouth, but you shall meditate in it day and night, that you may observe to do according to all that is written in it. For then you will make your way prosperous, and then you will have good success. (Josh. 1:8 NKJV)

By constantly meditating on the Word, we get to the point where we react according to the Word without even thinking about it. The Word of God becomes the central part of everything we think and do. Thoughts of failure or rejection or anger or anything else that we don't want are replaced by God's thoughts from His Word.

INTRODUCTION

Next we must confess the Word. It is to be not only in our hearts, but also in our mouths (Romans 10:8). The Word of God is to be spoken. In speaking about faith, Jesus told His followers that you must believe, but He also included speaking to the mountain.

For assuredly, I say to you, whoever says to this mountain, "Be removed and be cast into the sea," and does not doubt in his heart, but believes that those things he says will be done, he will have whatever he says. (Mark 11:23 NKJV)

We will have whatever we say. If we say negative things, if we speak

5

defeat and despair, then that is what we will have. If we say the Word of God, then we will have what the Word of God promises us. Proverbs 18:21 tells us "death and life are in the power of the tongue, and those who love it will eat its fruit."

Confessing God's Word is intended to be a tool for you to change your life. It provides a way of focusing on the Word of God and personalizing it to your own needs and circumstances. By speaking the Word out loud every day, even many times a day, you will accomplish the three things that are so important. You will fill yourself with the Word of God, hearing it over and over again. As you do that, it will be in your thinking constantly so that you will find yourself meditating on it. By reading the Word aloud, you will be speaking it, confessing it.

Confessing God's Word is intentionally small enough to carry with you wherever you go. Read it out loud, fill yourself with the Word, every day. If you are in the midst of a particular crisis, you can focus on that particular area of the Word. For example, if you are in need of healing, then you need to confess the healing scriptures every morning, in the middle of the day and every evening. It isn't that God needs to be convinced. He already wants to do good things for you. Rather, you need to become so convinced of the

CONFESSING *God's Word*

promises of God that there is no doubt anywhere in you. Speak the Word every chance you get. It will be healing to your body and health to your soul.

In Christ

Maureen Anderson

Maureen Anderson

CONFESSIONS

CONFESSING *God's Word*

CHAPTER ONE

BLESSING
Confessions

CONFESSING *God's Word*

God made me into a great nation in Christ. I am a blessing. (Gen. 12:2)

❧

I have received the names of God, and God has made my name great in Christ. (Eph. 3:14-15, Gen. 12:2)

❧

God will bless those who bless me and curse those who curse me. (Gen. 12:3)

❧

I am a blessing to all the peoples of the earth. (Gen. 12:3)

❧

Blessed be God Most High, for You deliver my enemies into my hands. (Gen. 14:20)

BLESSING CONFESSIONS

Lord, I am not afraid, for You are my shield and my very great reward. (Gen. 15:1)

☙

I have received all the blessings of Abraham in Christ. I will surely become a great and powerful nation, and all nations on earth will be blessed through me. (Gen. 18:18)

☙

Through my children all nations on earth will be blessed because I have obeyed You. (Gen. 22:18)

☙

The Lord has blessed me abundantly, and I have become wealthy. (Gen. 24:35)

CONFESSING *God's Word*

I planted seed and the same year reaped a hundredfold because the Lord has blessed me. (Gen. 26:12)

God Almighty, You bless me and make me fruitful and increase my numbers until I become a community of peoples. (Gen. 28:3)

I worship the Lord my God and His blessing is on my food and water. God has taken sickness away from me. (Ex. 23:25)

Thank You, God, for increasing me a thousand times and blessing me as You have promised. (Deut. 1:11)

BLESSING CONFESSIONS

God has given me land with large, flourishing cities I did not build. (Deut. 6:10)

❧

God has given me houses filled with all kinds of good things I did not provide. (Deut. 6:11)

❧

God has given me wells that I did not dig and vineyards and olive groves I did not plant. (Deut. 6:11)

❧

You love me, Lord; You bless me and increase me. (Deut. 7:13)

❧

Thank You, God, for You have given me the ability to produce wealth and so confirm Your covenant which You swore to my forefathers. (Deut. 8:18)

Confessing *God's Word*

I rule over many nations, but none will rule over me. (Deut. 15:6)

❧

I am set high above all the nations on the earth in Christ. (Deut. 28:1)

❧

The blessings come upon me and overtake me. (Deut. 28:2)

❧

I am blessed in the city and in the country. (Deut. 28:3)

❧

My descendants are blessed. (Deut. 28:4)

❧

All my possessions are blessed. (Deut. 28:4)

Blessing Confessions

I am blessed when I come in and when I go out. (Deut. 28:6)

✥

The Lord will grant that the enemies who rise up against me are defeated before me. The enemy comes in one direction and flees from me in seven. (Deut. 28:7)

✥

The Lord sends blessings on everything I put my hand to. The Lord blesses me in the land He has given me. (Deut. 28:8)

✥

The Lord establishes me as His holy people. (Deut. 28:9)

✥

I am called by the Name of the Lord. They will fear me. (Deut. 28:10)

Confessing *God's Word*

The Lord has granted me abundant prosperity. (Deut. 28:11)

❧

I will lend to many nations. I will borrow from none. (Deut. 28:12)

❧

The Lord has opened the heavens, the storehouse of his bounty, to bless all the work of my hands. (Deut. 28:12)

❧

The Lord has made me the head and not the tail. I am always at the top and never at the bottom. (Deut. 28:13)

❧

My delight is in the law of the Lord. On Your law I meditate day and night. I am like a tree planted by streams of water which yields its fruit in season and whose leaf does not wither. Whatever I do prospers. (Ps. 1:2-3)

❧

O Lord, You bless me for I have received the righteousness of Christ and You have surrounded me with favor as with a shield. (Ps. 5:12)

❧

I fear the Lord and the Lord instructs me in the way chosen for me. (Ps. 25:12)

❧

I spend my days in prosperity and my descendants will inherit the land. (Ps. 25:13)

❧

I fear the Lord and lack nothing. (Ps. 34:9)

Confessing *God's Word*

I am the righteous, and I am flourishing; I have abounding prosperity until the moon is no more. (Ps. 72:7)

❧

I am blessed because I fear the Lord, and I find great delight in God's commands. (Ps. 112:1)

❧

My children are mighty in the land, and the generation of the upright are blessed. (Ps. 112:2)

❧

Wealth and riches are in my house. (Ps. 112:3)

❧

I seek the prosperity of the Lord for the sake of the house of the Lord. (Ps. 122:9)

Blessing Confessions

I fear the Lord and walk in His ways. I eat the fruit of my labor. Blessings and prosperity will be mine. (Ps. 128:1-2)

❧

I love You, Lord, and You love me. I seek You and find You. With You are riches and honor, enduring wealth and prosperity. (Prov. 8:17-18)

❧

I have received the blessing of the Lord that has brought me wealth, and He adds no trouble to it. (Prov. 10:22)

❧

I am a generous person. I will prosper. (Prov. 11:25)

❧

I have received the righteousness of Christ. Prosperity is my reward. (Prov. 13:21)

CONFESSING *God's Word*

I have pursued righteousness and love. I have found life, prosperity, and honor. (Prov. 21:21)

❧

I have received the humility of Christ, and the fear of the Lord has brought me wealth and honor and life. (Prov. 22:4)

❧

God, You have given me wealth and possessions and enabled me to enjoy them. To accept my lot and be happy at my work—this is a gift from You. (Eccl. 5:19)

❧

I bring You the whole tithe into the storehouse that there is food in God's house. You, Lord Almighty, have thrown open the floodgates of heaven and poured out so much blessing that I do not have room enough for it. Lord, You rebuke the devourer for my sake so that he will not destroy the fruit of my ground, nor shall the vine fail to bear fruit for me in the field. (Mal. 3:10-11 NKJV)

❧

I am blessed. (2 Cor. 1:20)

❧

Jesus, You redeemed me in order that the blessings given to Abraham might come to me through You, Christ Jesus, so that by faith I might receive the promise of the Spirit. (Gal. 3:14)

❧

God has blessed me in the heavenly realms with every spiritual blessing in Christ. (Eph. 1:3)

Confessing *God's Word*

I am in Christ, far above all rule and all authority, power, and dominion and every title that can be given. (Eph. 1:21)

❧

I am not of this world. I am of the Kingdom of God, a citizen of Heaven. (Eph. 2:19)

❧

I am rescued from the dominion of darkness and I am brought into the Kingdom of His dear Son He loves. (Col. 1:13)

❧

I am redeemed from the empty way of life handed down from my forefathers by the precious blood of Christ. (1 Pet. 1:18-19)

CHAPTER TWO

Confessions of GOD'S WORD

Confessing *God's Word*

I am walking by faith and not by sight. (2 Cor. 5:7)

❧

I am rooted and grounded in love, because Christ dwells within me. (Eph. 3:17)

❧

I am complete in Christ. (Col. 2:10 NKJV)

❧

I am healed by the stripes of Jesus Christ. (1 Pet. 2:24)

❧

I am an imitator of God. (Eph. 5:1)

❧

I am a recreated being. Old things have passed away, and all things have become new. (2 Cor. 5:17 NKJV)

Confessions of God's Word

I am a son of God, and as a son, I am an heir of God through Christ. (Gal. 4:7)

※

I am reigning in life by Jesus Christ. (Rom. 5:17)

※

I am looking at the things that are not seen, for they are eternal. (2 Cor. 4:18)

※

I am casting down imaginations and every high thing that exalts itself against the knowledge of God. (2 Cor. 10:5a NKJV)

※

I am bringing into captivity every thought to make it obedient to Christ. (2 Cor. 10:5b NKJV)

27

CONFESSING *God's Word*

I am the workmanship of God, created in Christ. (Eph. 2:10)

❧

I am attending to God's Words, inclining my ear to His sayings. I keep them before my eyes; I keep them in the midst of my heart, for they are life unto me and health to all my flesh. (Prov. 4:20-22 NKJV)

❧

I am prosperous and in good health even as my soul prospers. (3 John 1:2)

❧

I am being transformed by the renewing of my mind, that I may know what is the good, acceptable and perfect will of God. (Rom. 12:2)

Confessions of God's Word

I am a branch of the Living Vine. (John 15:5)

⊰

I am more than a conqueror through Jesus Christ. (Rom. 8:37)

⊰

I am the salt of the earth, and I am the light of the world. (Matt. 5:13a, 14a)

⊰

I am strong in the Lord and in the power of His might. (Eph. 6:10)

⊰

I am created in God's glorious image and likeness. (Gen. 1:26-27)

⊰

I am full of His Spirit and divine power. (Eph. 5:18b)

CONFESSING *God's Word*

I am a spirit, so I have the fruit of His Spirit operating in my life: love, joy, peace, patience, kindness, goodness, faithfulness, gentleness and self-control. (Gal. 5:22-23a)

❧

I am a liberated person. Jesus said that I would know the truth and the truth would make me free! (John 8:32)

❧

I am standing fast in the liberty wherein Christ has made me free. (Gal. 5:1 NKJV)

❧

I am a righteous person, and I am reigning over God's creation now. (Rom. 5:17)

CONFESSIONS OF GOD'S WORD

I am expecting God to meet all my needs and to do superabundantly above all I dare ask, hope, dream or desire according to the power that works in me. (Eph. 3:20)

❧

Christ has been made worthy to receive power, riches, wisdom, strength, honor, glory and blessing. (Rev. 4:11)

❧

I am a disciplined person; I study God's Word daily. (2 Tim. 2:15 KJV)

❧

I am humbly submitting myself to the authority of His holy Word, for He and His Word are one. (John 1:1)

CONFESSING *God's Word*

I am God's property. I have been bought with the blood of the Lord Jesus Christ; therefore, I am free from the curse of the law. Sin, sickness, poverty, fear, doubt, worry, confusion and all that Satan represents shall not have dominion over me. (Gal. 3:13-14)

❧

I am obedient to His commandments. (1 John 2:3)

❧

I am strong and of good courage for the Lord my God is with me wherever I go. (Josh. 1:9)

❧

I am taking the shield of faith and quenching all the fiery darts of the enemy. (Eph. 6:16 NKJV)

Confessions of God's Word

I am of God and have overcome them (every spirit that does not confess that Jesus Christ has come in the flesh) because greater is He that is in me than he that is in the world. (1 John 4:4)

❧

I am praying and believing for God's desires and receiving what I ask for. (Mark 11:24)

❧

I am given exceedingly great and precious promises, and by them I am a partaker of God's divine nature. (2 Pet. 1:4)

❧

I am receiving all of my needs met according to God's riches in glory by Jesus Christ. (Phil. 4:19)

CONFESSING *God's Word*

I am the temple of the Holy Ghost. (1 Cor. 6:19)

❧

I am honoring the Lord with my substance and with the first fruits of all my increase, and God fills my barns with plenty. (Prov. 3:9, 10 KJV)

❧

I am led by the Spirit of God, and I walk after the Spirit. (Rom. 8:14)

❧

I am casting all of my cares upon God, because He cares for me. (1 Pet. 5:7)

❧

I am blessed with all spiritual blessings in Christ Jesus. (Eph. 1:3)

Confessions of God's Word

I am blessed when I come in and blessed when I go out. (Deut. 28:6)

❧

I am an heir of God and a joint-heir with Christ. (Rom. 8:17)

❧

I am increasing and abounding in love. (1 Thes. 3:12 NKJV)

❧

I am being made perfect in every good work to do God's will. (Heb. 13:21)

❧

I am given the Spirit of wisdom and revelation so I may know God better. (Eph. 1:17b)

❧

I have absolute freedom. The Son has made me free. (John 8:36)

35

CONFESSING *God's Word*

I am being filled with the knowledge of God's will through all spiritual wisdom and all spiritual understanding. I am living a life worthy of the Lord and pleasing Him in every way. I am bearing fruit in every good work, growing in the knowledge of God. (Col. 1:9, 10)

~

I have the anointing to teach me and lead me into all truth. The anointing of the Holy One abides in me. (1 John 2:27)

~

I have the ability to love everyone. The love of God has been poured out into my heart by the Holy Spirit. (Rom. 5:5)

CONFESSIONS OF GOD'S WORD

I have the outpouring of the Holy Spirit upon my life continually. (Acts 2:17)

❧

I have the presence of God each step I take. He will never leave me or forsake me. (Heb. 13:5,6)

❧

I have lionhearted boldness. The righteous are as bold as a lion. (Prov. 28:1)

❧

I am meditating on the Word day and night; I am observing to do according to all that is written therein. The Word says I am making my way prosperous, and I am having good success. (Josh. 1:8 NKJV)

Confessing *God's Word*

I am trusting in the Lord with all my heart and not leaning to my own understanding. In all my ways I am acknowledging Him, and He is directing my paths. (Prov. 3:5, 6)

❧

I have the peace of God, for the peace of God which passes all understanding shall keep my heart and mind through Christ Jesus our Lord. (Phil. 4:7)

❧

I have God, so I am set apart for God. (Ps. 4:3)

❧

I have His divine nature and by it have escaped the corruption in the world caused by evil desires. (2 Pet. 1:4)

CONFESSIONS OF GOD'S WORD

I have positive healings for the oppressed. I lay my hands on the sick, and they shall recover. (Mark 16:18)

❧

I am holy because He is Holy. (1 Pet. 1:16)

❧

I have all grace, abounding grace, saving grace, healing grace, baptizing grace, all sufficient grace. And God is able to make all grace abound toward me, that I, always having sufficiency in all things, may abound to every good work. (2 Cor. 9:8)

❧

I am holy, so I will see the Lord. (Heb. 12:14)

CONFESSING *God's Word*

I have the same Spirit that raised Christ from the dead. For the same Spirit that raised Christ from the dead dwells in me, and He shall give life to my mortal body. (Rom. 8:11)

❧

I have all His strength. For I can do all things through Christ who strengthens me. (Phil. 4:13)

❧

I move in dynamic deliverances. In the name of Jesus I cast out demons. (Mark 16:17)

❧

I have a life daily loaded with the benefits of the Lord. Blessed be the Lord, who daily loads me with benefits. (Ps. 68:19 NKJV)

CONFESSIONS OF GOD'S WORD

I have continual guidance because the Lord shall guide me continually. (Is. 58:11)

❧

I have Christ's life wherever I go. The thief comes only to steal, kill, and destroy... (John 10:10)

❧

I have eternal life, for Jesus' sheep hear His voice, and He gives them eternal life. (John 10:27, 28)

❧

I am free from fear, for the Lord my God will hold my right hand saying unto me, "Fear not." (Is. 41:13)

❧

I have special honor, for I serve Jesus. (John 12:26)

CONFESSING *God's Word*

I am supernaturally helped in every situation, for my help comes from the Lord who made heaven and earth. (Ps. 121:2)

❧

I have God's grace which teaches me to say, "No," to ungodliness and worldly passions, and to live a self-controlled, upright and godly life. (Tit. 2:11, 12)

❧

I am bountifully blessed financially, for he who sows bountifully shall also reap bountifully. (2 Cor. 9:6)

❧

God satisfies my desires with good things so that my youth is renewed like the eagle's. (Ps. 103:5)

CONFESSIONS OF GOD'S WORD

I have daily strength and an abundance of peace because the Lord bears my burdens. The Lord gives me strength and blesses me with peace. (Ps. 68:19)

❧

I have the assurance that my labor in the Lord is fruitful. (1 Cor. 15:58)

❧

Impossibilities are becoming realities, for I am linked up with God by divine birth. For with God nothing shall be impossible. (Luke 1:37)

❧

The Lord will give strength unto me, the Lord will bless me with peace. (Ps. 29:11)

Confessing *God's Word*

I have the mind of Christ. (1 Cor. 2:16b)

❧

I have light upon life's pathway, for I am following Jesus. (John 8:12)

❧

I have a spirit of power, love, and a sound mind. (2 Tim. 1:7b)

❧

No harm will befall me; no disaster will come near my tent. (Ps. 91:10)

❧

As God is, so am I in this world. (1 John 4:17b)

❧

The Lord will keep me from all harm; He will watch over my life. (Ps. 121:7)

CONFESSIONS OF GOD'S WORD

I have peace with my enemies, for
when a man's ways please the Lord,
He makes even his enemies to be at
peace with him. (Prov. 16:7)

CONFESSING *God's Word*

CHAPTER THREE

DESIRE
Confessions

Confessing *God's Word*

My desires are only good, for I am righteous. (Prov. 11:23 NKJV)

❧

God, You grant me according to my heart's desire and fulfill all my purposes. (Ps. 20:4 NKJV)

❧

When my desires are fulfilled, it is a tree of life to me. (Prov. 13:12 NKJV)

❧

God, You satisfy my desires with good things so that my youth is renewed like the eagle's. (Ps. 103:5)

❧

I delight myself in You, Lord, and You will give me the desires of my heart. (Ps. 37:4)

DESIRE CONFESSIONS

You have given me my heart's desire, and have not withheld the request of my lips. For You meet me with the blessings of goodness. You set a crown of pure gold upon my head. (Ps. 21:2-3 NKJV)

❧

You open Your hand and satisfy the desire of every living thing. (Ps. 145:16)

❧

God, You will fulfill my desires for I fear you... (Ps. 145:19)

❧

My desires will be granted, for I am righteous. (Prov. 10:24b NKJV)

❧

My desire accomplished is sweet to my soul... (Prov. 13:19 NKJV)

Confessing *God's Word*

Lord, You have been mindful of me; You will bless me. (Ps. 115:12 NKJV)

~

Your Word that goes out from my mouth; it will not return empty, but will accomplish what You desire and achieve the purpose for which it is sent. I will go out in joy and be led forth in peace; the mountains and the hills will burst into song before me, and all the trees of the field will clap their hands. (Is. 55: 11, 12)

~

God, I know the plans You have for me; plans to prosper me and not to harm me, plans to give me a hope and a future. (Jer. 29:11 NIV)

DESIRE CONFESSIONS

Lord, all my desire is before You, and my sighing is not hidden from You. (Ps. 38:9 NKJV)

❧

Lord, You have heard the desire of the humble; You will prepare my heart. (Ps. 10:17 NKJV)

❧

Now to You, God, who is able to do exceedingly abundantly above all that I ask or think, according to the power that works in me. (Eph. 3:20 NKJV)

❧

I am diligent, and my desires are fully satisfied. (Prov.13:4)

Confessing *God's Word*

CHAPTER FOUR

FAVOR
Confessions

CONFESSING *God's Word*

Lord, You are with me; You showed me kindness and granted me favor in the eyes of [other person's name]. (Gen. 39:21)

☙

I am abounding with the favor of You, Lord, and I am full of Your blessings. (Deut. 33:23)

☙

Look upon my shield, O God; look with favor on Your anointed one. (Ps. 84:9)

☙

I continue to grow in favor with You, Lord, and with men. (1 Sam. 2:26)

☙

I win favor with everyone who sees me. (Esth. 2:15c)

Favor Confessions

Lord, You look on me with favor, You make me fruitful, You increase my numbers, and You will keep Your covenant with me. (Lev. 26:9)

❧

O Lord, You bless me and surround me with Your favor as with a shield. (Ps. 5:12)

❧

Foreigners will rebuild my walls, and their kings will serve me. In favor God, You will show me compassion. (Is. 60:10)

❧

You will arise and have compassion on me, for it is time to show favor to me. The appointed time has come. (Ps. 102:13)

Confessing *God's Word*

I have found You, Lord. I found life, and I receive favor from You, Lord. (Prov. 8:35)

❧

O Lord, You favor me. You made my mountain stand firm. (Ps. 30:7)

❧

I am not afraid, for I have found favor with God. (Luke 1:30)

❧

God, Your favor lasts a lifetime. (Ps. 30:5a)

❧

God, You are my glory and strength, and by Your favor you exalt my horn. (Ps. 89:17)

❧

I seek the favor of the Lord my God. (Exod. 32:11a)

FAVOR CONFESSIONS

I find favor in the eyes of the Lord. (Gen. 6:8)

❧

Lord, You have granted me life and favor. (Job 10:12 NKJV)

❧

I am proclaiming the year of the Lord's favor. (Is. 61:2)

❧

I am growing in wisdom and stature, and in favor with God and men. (Luke 2:52)

❧

Now God, You have caused (other person's name) to show favor and sympathy to me. (Dan. 1:9)

Confessing *God's Word*

I fear You Lord, and I seek Your favor.
(Jer. 26:19b)

~

He who finds a wife finds what is good
and receives favor from the Lord.
(Prov. 18:22)

~

If you are pleased with me, God, teach
me Your ways so I may know You and
continue to find favor with You. (Ex.
33:13a)

~

You made me a little lower than the
heavenly beings and crowned me
with glory and honor (favor). (Ps. 8:5)

~

O Lord, You give me favor and honor.
(Ps. 84:11)

Favor Confessions

The favor of the Lord, my God, rests upon me. (Ps. 90:17)

❧

God said, "I know you by name and you have found favor with Me." (Ex. 33:12b)

❧

O Lord, You are concerned for me, and You will look on me with favor. (Ez. 36:9)

❧

I am a good person, and I have obtained favor from You, Lord. (Prov. 12:2)

❧

The Lord looked with favor on my offering. (Gen. 4:4b)

CONFESSING *God's Word*

The Lord makes His face shine upon me (favors me) and is gracious to me. (Num. 6:25)

On earth, peace to me on whom God's favor rests. (Luke 2:14b)

CHAPTER FIVE

HEALING
Confessions

CONFESSING *God's Word*

You are the Lord that healeth me. (Ex. 15:26b NKJV)

❧

For You, Lord, are my physician. (Leeser)

❧

You are the Lord my life-giver. (BE)

❧

You are the Lord my healer. (NEB)

❧

You are Yahweh the physician. (Rotherham)

❧

And I give worship to the Lord my God, who will send a blessing on my bread and on my water. And You will take all disease away from me. (Ex. 23:25 BE)

HEALING CONFESSIONS

…You, Lord, will bring me only health. (Knox)

※

For You, Lord, make me immune to them (diseases). (SG)

※

You, Jehovah, are healing me. (Young)

※

Bless the Lord, O my soul, and forget not all his benefits: Who forgiveth all my iniquities; who healeth all my diseases. (Ps. 103:2-3 KJV)

※

He sent His Word, and healed me, and delivered me from my destructions. (Ps. 107:20)

Confessing *God's Word*

And the Lord will take away from me all sickness, and will put none of the evil diseases of Egypt, which I know, upon me; but will lay them upon all them that hate me. (Deut. 7:15 KJV)

❧

Why art thou cast down, O my soul, and why art thou disquieted within me? Hope thou in God, for I shall yet praise Him, who is the health of my countenance, and my God. (Ps. 42:11 KJV)

❧

And I shall serve the Lord my God, and He shall bless my bread, and my water; and the Lord will take sickness away from my midst. (Ex. 23:25 KJV)

HEALING CONFESSIONS

You, Lord, will free me from disease. (Moffatt)

✦

You, Lord, have turned aside sickness from my heart. (Young)

✦

...and keep sickness away from my company. (Knox)

✦

He sent out His word, and it healed me, and from my corruptions it freed me! (Ps. 107:20)

✦

I attend to God's Words; I incline my ear unto God's sayings. I let them not depart from my eyes. I keep them in the midst of my heart. For they are life unto me because I found them, and health to all my flesh. (Prov. 4:20-22 Fenton)

CONFESSING *God's Word*

I let them penetrate deep within my heart. (LB)

❧

I master them; they will bring life and healing to my whole being. (Knox)

❧

...and to all my body a healing. (Leeser)

❧

...to every part of my flesh they bring healing. (Rotherham)

❧

O Lord my God, I cried unto thee, and thou hast healed me. (Ps. 30:2 KJV)

❧

You, Lord, pardon all my guilt and heal all my suffering. (NEB)

HEALING CONFESSIONS

He takes away all my diseases. (BE)

❧

...Who is healing all my diseases. (Young)

❧

He sent His word to heal me and preserve my life. (Ps. 107:20 Moffatt)

❧

...and delivereth them from their graves. (Leeser)

❧

Reckless words pierce like a sword, but the tongue of the wise brings healing. (Prov. 12:18)

❧

A reckless tongue wounds like a sword, but there is healing power in thoughtful words. (Moffatt)

Confessing *God's Word*

Thoughtless words can wound as deeply as any sword, but wisely spoken words can heal. (GN)

❧

There are some whose uncontrolled talk is like the wounds of a sword, but the tongue of the wise makes one well again. (BE)

❧

But it was my pain He took, and my diseases were put on Him. While to me He seemed as one diseased on whom God's punishment had come. (Is. 53:4 BE)

❧

Yet surely my sicknesses He carried, and as for my pains, He bore the burden of them. (Rotherham)

HEALING CONFESSIONS

But in fact it was my sicknesses He was carrying, my pains He was loaded with. (Byington)

※

With His stripes I am healed. (Is. 53:5)

※

But only my diseases did He bear Himself, and my pains He carried. (Is. 53:4 Leeser)

※

Yet it was my sicknesses that He bore, my pains that He carried. (SG)

※

Through His bruises was healing granted to me. (Is. 53:5 Leeser)

Confessing *God's Word*

Surely my diseases did He bear, and my pains He carried. (Is. 53:4 Masoretic OT)

᪐

By His stripes there is healing for me. (Is. 53:5 Rotherham)

᪐

The chastisement to give me soundness came on Him, and by His stripes I got healing. (Byington)

᪐

The blows that fell to Him have brought me healing. (Moffatt)

᪐

I am healed by the punishment He suffered, made whole by the blows He received. (GN)

Healing Confessions

The chastisement needful to obtain peace and well-being for me was upon Him, and with the stripes that wounded Him I am healed and made whole. (AMP)

~

By His bruise there is healing to me. (Young)

~

A merry heart doeth good like a medicine, but a broken spirit drieth the bones. (Prov. 17:22 KJV)

~

Being cheerful keeps me healthy. (GN)

~

A glad heart is excellent medicine; a spirit depressed wastes the bones away. (Jerusalem)

Confessing *God's Word*

A broken spirit makes one sick.
(LB)

❧

A happy heart is a healing medicine…
(SG)

❧

A glad heart makes a healthy body.
(BE)

❧

A glad heart helps and heals.
(Moffatt)

❧

The best medicine is a cheerful heart.
(Fenton)

❧

A joyful heart worketh an excellent
cure. (Rotherham)

Healing Confessions

A cheerful heart makes a quick recovery; it is crushed spirits that waste a man's frame. (Knox)

~

God anointed Jesus of Nazareth with the Holy Ghost and with power, who went about doing good and healing all who were oppressed of the devil, for God was with Him. (Acts 10:38 KJV)

~

...all who were harassed by the devil. (Moffatt)

~

...healing all who were under the power of the devil. (NIV)

Confessing *God's Word*

God equipped Him with the Holy Spirit and power, who passed through our midst acting nobly and healing all those who were lorded over by the devil. (Jordan)

❧

...curing all who were crushed by the power of the devil... (WEY)

❧

...healing all that were overpowered by the devil. (NB)

❧

...curing all those who were under tyranny of the devil. (Barclay)

❧

...healing everyone in the devil's clutches. (Rieu)

HEALING CONFESSIONS

But if the Spirit of Him that raised up Jesus from the dead dwells in me, He that raised up Christ from the dead shall also quicken my mortal body by His Spirit that dwelleth in me. (Rom. 8:11 KJV)

≈

If the Spirit of God, of Him who raised Jesus from the dead, has its home in me, then He who raised the Messiah Jesus from the dead will thrill with a new life my very body the mortal body of mine by the agency of His own Spirit, which now has its home in me. (Way)

≈

...will also create life in my mortal body. (Godbey)

Confessing *God's Word*

Christ ransomed me from the curse of the law by taking that curse upon Himself for my sake. (Gal. 3:13 TNT)

❧

If the Spirit of God, of Him who raised Jesus from the dead, has taken possession of me, He who raised Christ Jesus from the dead will also give my mortal body life through His Spirit that has now taken possession of me. (Rom. 8:11 SG)

❧

Christ hath redeemed me from the curse of the law, being made a curse for me; for it is written, cursed is everyone that hangeth on a tree. (Gal. 3:13 KJV)

Healing Confessions

Christ ransomed me from the curse pronounced in the law... (20th C)

❧

Now, Christ bought me off the curse of the law at the cost of being accursed for my sake. (Wand)

❧

Christ has purchased my freedom. (WEY)

❧

I do not forget Your teaching, Lord, but I keep Your commands in my heart, for they will prolong my life many years and bring me prosperity. (Prov. 3:1-2)

❧

God has given me power to tread on serpents and scorpions, and over all the power of the enemy, and nothing shall by any means hurt me. (Luke 10:19 KJV)

And when Jesus saw her, He called her to Him, and said unto her, "Woman, thou art loosed from thine infirmity." (Luke 13:12 KJV)

"...thou art delivered." (Douay)

"...you are freed from your sickness." (NASNT)

"...thou hast been loosed..." (Marshall)

"...you are made free from your disease." (BE)

HEALING CONFESSIONS

"…you are now rid of your infirmity."
(Norlie)

❧

"…you are set free from your infirmity."
(NIV)

❧

"…you are freed from your disease."
(PE)

❧

"Lady, you have been freed from your
weakness." (Jordan)

❧

But unto me, who fears God's name
shall the Sun of Righteousness arise
with healing in His wings; and I shall
go forth, and grow up as a calf of the
stall. (Mal. 4:2)

Confessing *God's Word*

...with healing in its beams. (ML)

❧

I neither give place to the devil. (Eph. 4:27)

❧

I stop giving the devil a place or opportunity in my life. (Williams)

❧

...and I do not give the devil a chance. (TNT)

❧

Giving thanks unto the Father, which hath made me meet to be a partaker of the inheritance of the saints in light. (Col. 1:12 KJV)

CHAPTER SIX

HOLY SPIRIT
Confessions

Confessing *God's Word*

Holy Spirit, I want to be moved by You. (Luke 2:27)

⁓

Holy Spirit, I drink of You. (1 Cor. 12:13)

⁓

Holy Spirit, lead me into all truth. (John 16:13)

⁓

Holy Spirit, speak what You hear, and tell me what is yet to come. (John 16:13)

⁓

Holy Spirit, I choose to pray in a tongue, and I pray to interpret it. (1 Cor. 14:13-15)

⁓

Holy Spirit, give me life. (2 Cor. 3:6; John 6:63)

HOLY SPIRIT CONFESSIONS

Holy Spirit, teach me what I should say. (Luke 12:12)

❧

Holy Spirit, I have the Word of God and You without limit. (John 3:34)

❧

Holy Spirit, teach me all things. (John 14:26)

❧

Holy Spirit, I receive power from You. (Acts 1:8)

❧

Holy Spirit, testify to me about Jesus. (Rev. 19:10, John 15:26, 1 John 5:6)

❧

Holy Spirit, convict me of sin, of righteousness, and judgment yet to come. (John 16:8-11)

Confessing *God's Word*

Holy Spirit, You bring freedom. (2 Cor. 3:17)

❧

Holy Spirit, I live by You. (Gal. 5:16)

❧

Holy Spirit, I sow to please You, and I reap eternal life. (Gal. 6:8)

❧

Holy Spirit, be poured out on me. (Acts 2:17)

❧

Holy Spirit, show me what God has prepared for me because I love God. (1 Cor. 2:9-10)

❧

Holy Spirit, give me Your thoughts, Your words, and Your expressions. (1 Cor. 2:13)

84

HOLY SPIRIT CONFESSIONS

Holy Spirit, give me understanding of what God has freely given me. (1 Cor. 2:12)

❧

God has anointed me with You, Holy Spirit, and power. I go about doing good and healing all who are under the power of the devil. (Acts 10:38)

❧

Holy Spirit, I embrace and draw from the love of God that You put in my heart. (Rom. 5:5)

❧

Holy Spirit, anoint me to preach good news to the poor, to proclaim freedom for the prisoners, and recovery of sight for the blind, to release the oppressed. (Luke 4:18)

CONFESSING *God's Word*

Holy Spirit, fill me, and speak boldly through me. (Acts 4:31)

❧

Holy Spirit, strengthen and encourage me. (Acts 9:31)

❧

Holy Spirit, circumcise my heart. (Rom. 2:29)

❧

Holy Spirit, teach me to serve by the Spirit. (Rom. 7:6)

❧

Holy Spirit, I want my mind to be set on what You desire. (Rom. 8:5)

❧

Holy Spirit, be my counselor, comforter, strengthener, and encourager. (John 15:26, 1 Cor. 14:3)

Holy Spirit Confessions

Holy Spirit, write on my heart and mind. (2 Cor. 3:3)

❧

Holy Spirit, guide me into all truth. (John 16:13, Rom. 8:14, Gal. 5:18)

❧

Holy Spirit, I pray in the Spirit to be built up in my most holy faith. (Jude 20)

❧

Holy Spirit, give me ears to hear what You are saying to the Church. (Rev. 2:7)

❧

Holy Spirit, fill me with Your presence. (Eph. 5:18)

❧

God sends me and I speak His words. Holy Spirit, I have You without limit. (John 3:34)

CONFESSING *God's Word*

CHAPTER SEVEN

LOVE
Confessions

CONFESSING *God's Word*

God, You have poured out your love into my heart by the Holy Spirit, whom you have given to me. (Rom. 5:5)

❧

God, You have demonstrated Your own love for me in that while I was still a sinner, Christ died for me. (Rom. 5:8)

❧

For I know in all things, God works for the good of me who loves Him, who has been called according to His purpose. (Rom. 8:28)

❧

Nothing shall separate me from the love of Christ, not trouble or hardship or persecution or famine or nakedness or danger or sword. (Rom. 8:35)

LOVE CONFESSIONS

God's love in me is sincere. I hate what is evil; I cling to what is good. (Rom. 12:9)

❧

I let no debt remain outstanding, except the continuing debt to love others, for I love my fellowman and fulfill the law. (Rom. 13:8)

❧

I am devoted to others in brotherly love. (Rom. 12:10)

❧

I abide in God's love so I do no harm to my neighbor. (Rom. 13:10)

❧

In the love of the Spirit, I ask others to join me in my struggles by praying to God for me. (Rom.15:30)

Confessing *God's Word*

No eye has seen, no ear has heard, and no mind has conceived what God has prepared for me who loves Him. (1 Cor. 2:9)

❧

God has revealed what He has prepared for me by His Spirit. (1 Cor. 2:10a)

❧

Praise God that the Spirit searches all things even the deep things of God. (1 Cor. 2:10b)

❧

Knowledge will puff me up, but love will build me up. (1 Cor. 8:1b)

❧

I eagerly desire the greater gifts, love. (1 Cor. 12:31)

Love Confessions

I walk in love, so I am patient, I am kind, I do not envy, I do not boast, I am not proud. I am not rude, I am not self-seeking, I am not easily angered, I keep no record of wrongs. I do not delight in evil; I do rejoice with the truth. (1 Cor. 13:4-6)

❧

Love in my life always protects. Love in my life always trusts. Love in my life always hopes. Love in my life always perseveres. (1 Cor. 13:7)

❧

Love in my life never fails. (1 Cor. 13:8a)

❧

Faith, hope, and love remain, but the greatest of these is love. (1 Cor. 13:13)

CONFESSING *God's Word*

I follow the way of God's love. (1 Cor. 14:1)

❧

I do everything in love. (1 Cor. 16:14)

❧

For Christ's love compels me. (2 Cor. 5:14)

❧

I show these people the proof of my love…so that the churches can see it. (2 Cor. 8:24)

❧

May the grace of the Lord Jesus Christ, and the love of God, and the fellowship of the Holy Spirit be with me and you all. (2 Cor. 13:14)

Love Confessions

The only thing that counts is faith expressing itself through love. (Gal. 5:6)

❧

I do not use my freedom to indulge the sinful nature; rather I serve others in love. (Gal. 5:13)

❧

I love my neighbor as myself. (Gal. 5:14)

❧

But the fruit of the Spirit is love, joy, peace, patience, kindness, goodness, faithfulness, gentleness and self-control. (Gal. 5:22-23a)

❧

For He chose me in Him before the creation of the world to be holy and blameless in His sight in love. (Eph. 1:4)

CONFESSING *God's Word*

I have love for all the saints. (Eph. 1:15)

≈

But because of His great love for me, God, who is rich in mercy, made me alive with Christ, even when I was dead in transgressions; it is by grace I have been saved. (Eph. 2:4-5)

≈

I am being rooted and established in love, and I have the power, together with all the saints, to grasp how wide and long and high and deep is the love of Christ, and to know this love that surpasses knowledge, that I may be filled to the measure of all the fullness of God. (Eph. 3:17-19)

Love Confessions

I am completely humble and gentle; I am patient, bearing with others in love. (Eph. 4:2)

☙

I speak the truth in love, so I will in all things grow up into Him who is the Head, that is, Christ. (Eph. 4:15)

☙

From Him the whole body, joined and held together by every supporting ligament, grows and builds itself up in love, as each part does its work. (Eph. 4:16)

☙

I choose to live a life of love, just as Christ loved me and gave Himself up for me as a fragrant offering and sacrifice to God. (Eph. 5:2)

Confessing *God's Word*

Grace to me who loves our Lord Jesus Christ with an undying love. (Eph. 6:24)

❧

My labor is prompted by love. (1 Thes. 1:3)

❧

God's love comforts me. (Phil. 2:1)

❧

My love abounds more and more in knowledge and depth of insight, so that I may be able to discern what is best and may be pure and blameless until the day of Christ filled with the fruit of righteousness that comes through Jesus Christ to the glory and praise of God. (Phil. 1:9–11)

LOVE CONFESSIONS

I am one of God's chosen people, holy and dearly loved, and I clothe myself with compassion, kindness, humility, gentleness and patience. I bear with others and forgive whatever grievances I may have against another. I forgive as the Lord has forgiven me. (Col. 3:12-13)

~

God is not unjust; He will not forget my work and the love I have shown Him as I have helped His people and continue to help them. (Heb. 6:10)

~

The Lord directs my heart into God's love and Christ's perseverance. (2 Thes. 3:5)

CONFESSING *God's Word*

I have faith and love that spring from the hope that is stored up for me in heaven. (Col. 1:5)

❧

May the Lord make my love increase and overflow for everyone else. (1 Thes. 3:12)

❧

Thank You, God, for You teach me to love others. (1 Thes. 4:9)

❧

Since I belong to the day, I am self-controlled, putting on faith and love as a breastplate and the hope of salvation as a helmet. (1 Thes. 5:8)

❧

Father, I respect those who work hard among me, who are over me in the Lord and who admonish me, I hold them in the highest regard in love because of their work. I live in peace with others. (1 Thes. 5:12-13)

❧

My love for everyone is increasing. (2 Thes. 1:3)

❧

God wants me to love from a pure heart and a good conscience and a sincere faith. (1 Tim. 1:5)

❧

The grace of our Lord was poured out on me abundantly, along with faith and love that are in Christ Jesus. (1 Tim. 1:14)

❧

I set an example for the believers in speech, in life, in love, in faith and in purity. (1 Tim. 4:12)

Confessing *God's Word*

I pursue righteousness, godliness, faith, love, endurance and gentleness. (1 Tim. 6:11)

❧

For God did not give me a spirit of timidity (or fear), but a spirit of power, of love and of self-discipline (or a sound mind). (2 Tim. 1:7)

❧

I flee the evil desires of youth, and pursue righteousness, faith, love and peace, along with those who call on the Lord out of a pure heart. (2 Tim. 2:22)

❧

There is no fear in love, but perfect love drives out fear, because fear has to do with punishment. I have been made perfect in love. (1 John 4:18)

LOVE CONFESSIONS

I know I love the children of God, by loving God and carrying out His commands. (1 John 5:2)

⁓

I consider how I may spur others on toward love and good deeds. (Heb. 10:24)

⁓

I am blessed because I persevere under trials, because when I have stood the test, I will receive the crown of life that God has promised to those who love Him. (James 1:12)

⁓

I love so I have been born of God and I know God. (1 John 4:7)

CONFESSING *God's Word*

I obey His word so God's love is truly made complete in me. (1 John 2:5)

❧

Father, how great is Your love for me that You have lavished on me, that I should be called Your child. (1 John 3:1)

❧

I know that I have passed from death to life, because I love the brothers. (1 John 3:14)

❧

This is love, that I lay down my life for the brothers. (1 John 3:16)

❧

I do not love with words or tongue but with actions and in truth. (1 John 3:18)

LOVE CONFESSIONS

I love others, God lives in me and his love is made complete in me. (1 John 4:12)

I know and rely on the love God has for me; God is Love. I live in love, so I live in God and God in me. (1 John 4:16)

I walk in love. (2 John 6)

I inherit the kingdom the Lord has promised to me because I love Him. (James 2:5)

Though I have not seen Him, I love Him; and even though I do not see Him now, I believe in Him and I am filled with an inexpressible and glorious joy. (1 Pet. 1:8)

Confessing *God's Word*

I have purified myself by obeying the truth so that I have sincere love for the brothers, and I love others deeply, from the heart. (1 Pet. 1:22)

❧

Above all, I love others deeply, because love covers over a multitude of sins. (1 Pet. 4:8)

❧

I greet others with a kiss of love. (1 Pet. 5:14)

CHAPTER EIGHT

Power of
LAUGHTER

Confessing *God's Word*

I will laugh at destruction (oppression, devastation, violence, injustice) and famine. (Job 5:22)

❧

They gather together against the Lord and against His anointed one. The One enthroned in heaven laughs, and so do I. (Ps. 2:2-4)

❧

My heart is cheerful, and it is good medicine to me. (Prov. 17:22a)

❧

I laugh at the days to come. I fill my future with laughter. (Prov. 31:25)

❧

God fills my mouth with laughter and my lips with shouts of joy. (Job 8:21)

POWER OF LAUGHTER

He will yet fill my mouth with laughter and my lips with rejoicing. (Job 8:21 AMP)

❧

The Lord and I laugh at the wicked, for we know their day is coming. (Ps. 37:13)

❧

This is the day that the Lord has made; I will rejoice and be glad in it. (Ps. 118:24)

❧

This day is sacred to my Lord. I will not grieve for the joy of the Lord is my strength. (Neh. 8:10b)

❧

I am the Lord's disciple, filled with joy and with the Holy Spirit. (Acts 13:52)

God is my daily delight; God is always laughing before me, laughing in my inhabited world, and I am God's delight. (Prov. 8:30-31)

❧

For the kingdom of God is not a matter of eating and drinking, but of righteousness, peace and joy in the Holy Spirit, because if I serve Christ in this way, it is pleasing to God and approved by men. (Rom. 14:17-18)

❧

My mouth is filled with laughter and my tongue with songs of joy. Then it is said among the nations, "The Lord has done great things for me." (Ps. 126:2)

POWER OF LAUGHTER

I have loved righteousness and hated wickedness; therefore God, my God, has set me above my companions by anointing me with the oil of joy. (Heb.1:9)

Confessing *God's Word*

CHAPTER NINE

PREACHING
Confessions

CONFESSING *God's Word*

I devoted myself to the study and observance of the law of the Lord and to teaching its decrees and its laws to God's people. (Ezra 7:10)

❧

O God's people, hear God's teaching; listen to the words of God's mouth. (Ps. 78:1)

❧

Do not forget my teaching, but keep my commands in your heart. (Prov. 3:1)

❧

This teaching is a light. (Prov. 6:23a)

❧

When the crowd heard this, they were astonished at my teaching. (Matt. 22:33)

Preaching Confessions

I go about teaching in their churches, preaching the Gospel of the kingdom, and healing every disease and sickness among the people. (Matt. 4:23)

❦

When I had finished saying these things, the crowds were amazed at my teachings because I taught as one who had authority. (Matt. 7:28-29)

❦

They were amazed at my teachings about the Lord. (Acts 13:12b)

❦

God is my witness whom I serve with my whole heart in preaching the Gospel of His Son. (Rom. 1:9)

I came out, saw a great multitude and was moved with compassion for them because they were like sheep not having a shepherd. So I began to teach them many things. (Mark 6:34)

~

I devote myself to the public teaching of scripture, to preaching and to teaching. (1 Tim. 4:13)

~

All scripture is God-breathed and is useful for teaching, rebuking, correcting, and training me in righteousness. (2 Tim. 3:16)

~

I devoted myself exclusively to preaching and testifying that Jesus was the Christ. (Acts 18:5)

PREACHING CONFESSIONS

I went through all the towns and villages [cities] teaching in their churches, preaching the good news of the kingdom and healing every disease and sickness. (Matt. 9:35)

❦

I open my mouth, and God fills it. (Ps. 81:10b)

❦

The Sovereign Lord has given me an instructed tongue to know the word that sustains the weary. (Is. 50:4)

❦

My tongue is a pen of a skillful writer. (Ps. 45:1b)

❦

God has anointed my lips with grace. (Ps. 45:2)

Confessing *God's Word*

I let the Word of Christ dwell in me richly as I teach and admonish others with all wisdom and gratitude in my heart to God. (Col. 3:16)

❧

I preach the Word of God, and I am prepared in season and out of season, to correct, to rebuke, and to encourage with great patience and careful instruction. (2 Tim. 4:2)

❧

My teaching is of the wise and is a fountain of life turning people away from the snare of death. (Prov. 13:14)

❧

The Spirit of the Sovereign Lord is upon me, because the Lord has anointed me to preach good news to the poor. He has sent me to bind up the brokenhearted, to proclaim freedom for the captives, and release from darkness the prisoners, to proclaim the year of the Lord's favor and the day of vengeance of our God, to comfort all who mourn, and provide for those who grieve in Zion, to bestow on them a crown of beauty instead of ashes, the oil of gladness instead of mourning, and the garment of praise for the spirit of despair. They will be called oaks of righteousness, a planting of the Lord for the display of His splendor. (Is. 61:1-3)

❧

All spoke well of me and were amazed at the gracious words that came from my lips. (Luke 4:22a)

119

Confessing *God's Word*

All the people were amazed and said to each other, "What is this teaching?" With authority and power I give orders to evil spirits and they come out! And the news about me spread throughout the surrounding area, for my teachings came from God. (Luke 4: 36-37)

❧

Day after day in the church and from house to house I have never stopped teaching and proclaiming the good news that Jesus is the Christ. (Acts 5:42)

❧

I proclaim Jesus, admonish, and teach everyone with all wisdom so that I may present everyone perfect in Christ Jesus. (Col. 1:28)

Preaching Confessions

Jesus gave me all authority to teach them to obey everything He has commanded me. (Matt. 28:18, 20)

CONFESSING *God's Word*

CHAPTER TEN

PROSPERITY
Confessions

Confessing *God's Word*

My God shall supply all my needs. (Phil. 4:19)

❧

Above all things, God wishes that I may prosper. (3 John 2 KJV)

❧

For the Lord...has pleasure in the prosperity of me, His servant. (Ps. 35:27 AMP)

❧

The Lord shall make me plenteous in goods, in the fruit of my body, and in the fruit of my cattle, and in the fruit of my ground. (Deut. 28:11 KJV)

❧

For the earth is the Lord's, and the fullness thereof. (1 Cor. 10:26 KJV)

Prosperity Confessions

The Lord shall command the blessing upon me…in all that I set my hand to. (Deut. 28:8 NKJV)

❧

For the Lord God says, "The barrel of meal shall not waste, neither shall the cruse of oil fail." (1 Kings 17:14 KJV)

❧

I seek first the expansion of God's kingdom worldwide, and all these things shall be added unto me. (Matt. 6:33)

❧

I shall remember the Lord my God: for it is He who gives me power to get wealth. (Deut. 8:18 KJV)

Confessing *God's Word*

I shall make my way prosperous, and I shall have good success. (Josh. 1:8 KJV)

❧

The Lord is my shepherd; I shall not want. (Ps. 23:1 KJV)

❧

No good thing will He withhold from me who walks uprightly. (Ps. 84:11 KJV)

❧

The blessing of the Lord brings me wealth. (Prov. 10:22)

❧

Blessed am I who fears the Lord, who delights greatly in His commandments. Wealth and riches shall be in my house. (Ps. 112:1-3 KJV)

Prosperity Confessions

There is no one who has left house, or brothers, or sisters, or father, or mother, or wife, or children, or lands, for my sake, and the Gospel's, but she or he shall receive an hundredfold now in this time, (houses, and loved ones and lands) and in the world to come eternal life. (Mark 10:29, 30 KJV)

≈

All the earth is mine. (Ex. 19:5 KJV)

≈

I am a faithful person, and I shall abound with blessings. (Prov. 28:20)

≈

Blessed is the Lord, who daily loads me with benefits. (Ps. 68:19a KJV)

Confessing *God's Word*

I keep...the words of this covenant... that I may prosper in all that I do. (Deut. 29:9 KJV)

❦

Riches and wealth are the gift of God. (Eccl. 5:19 KJV)

❦

The silver is mine and the gold is mine. (Hag. 2:8)

❦

For every beast of the forest is mine, and the cattle upon a thousand hills. (Ps. 50:10 KJV)

❦

O Lord, how manifold are Your works...the earth is full of Your riches...You open Your hand; they are filled with good things. (Ps. 104:24, 28 KJV)

Prosperity Confessions

The Lord will open to me His good treasure. (Deut. 28:12 KJV)

❧

I walk in His ways…that I may prosper in all I do and wherever I turn myself. (1 Kings 2:3)

❧

The land is mine. (Lev. 25:23)

❧

Jesus has come that I may have life, and that I may have it more abundantly. (John 10:10 KJV)

❧

Those that seek me early shall find me. Riches and honor are with me; yes, durable riches and righteousness… that I may cause those that love me to inherit substance; and I will fill their treasures. (Prov. 8:17, 18, 21 KJV)

CONFESSING *God's Word*

CHAPTER ELEVEN

Names of GOD

CONFESSING *God's Word*

ELOHIM — Miracle strength, the Creator, creating.

❧

EL SHADDAI — Mighty blessings, God Almighty.

❧

ADONAI — In control, the One in charge.

❧

JEHOVAH — Lord, always present.

❧

JEHOVAH JIREH — Jehovah's provision shall be seen. Provider, takes care of our needs.

❧

JEHOVAH M'KADDESH — Jehovah who sanctifies, establishes us holy and godly.

NAMES OF GOD

JEHOVAH NISSI — Jehovah my Banner, victory in defeated places.

❧

JEHOVAH ROPHE — Jehovah heals, Healer.

❧

JEHOVAH ROHI — Jehovah my Shepherd, revealer of His personality.

❧

JEHOVAH SHALOM — Jehovah is Peace, peace inside and out.

❧

JEHOVAH SHAMMAH — Jehovah is there, abiding with us.

❧

JEHOVAH TSIDKENU — Jehovah our righteousness; Jehovah our right thoughts and right actions.

133

Confessing *God's Word*

SCRIPTURE
PRAYERS

CONFESSING *God's Word*

CHAPTER TWELVE

General Scripture
PRAYERS

Confessing *God's Word*

The law of the Lord is perfect, reviving the soul. The statutes of the Lord are trustworthy, making wise the simple. The precepts of the Lord are right, giving joy to the heart. The commands of the Lord are radiant, giving light to the eyes. The fear of the Lord is pure, enduring forever. The ordinances of the Lord are sure and altogether righteous. They are more precious than gold, than much pure gold; they are sweeter than honey, than honey from the comb. By them is your servant warned; in keeping them there is great reward. Who can discern his errors? Forgive my hidden faults. Keep your servant also from willful sins; may they not rule over me. Then will I be blameless, innocent of great transgression. May the words of my mouth and the meditation of my heart be pleasing in Your sight, O Lord, my Rock and my Redeemer. (Ps. 19:7-14)

❧

With this in mind, we constantly pray for you, that our God may count you worthy of His calling, and that by His power He may fulfill every good purpose of yours and every act prompted by your faith. We pray this so that the name of our Lord Jesus may be glorified in you, and you in Him, according to the grace of our God and the Lord Jesus Christ. (2 Thes. 1:11-12)

❧

And pray that we may be delivered from wicked and evil men, for not everyone has faith. But the Lord is faithful, and He will strengthen and protect you from the evil one. (2 Thes. 3:2)

❧

I pray that out of his glorious riches He may strengthen you with power through His Spirit in your inner being, so that Christ may dwell in your hearts through faith. And I pray that you, being rooted and established in love, may have power, together with all the saints, to grasp how wide and long and high and deep is the love of Christ, and to know this love that surpasses knowledge—that you may be filled to the measure of all the fullness of God. Now to Him who is able to do immeasurably more than all we ask or imagine, according to His power that is at work within us. (Eph. 3:16-20)

I keep asking that the God of our
Lord Jesus Christ, the glorious
Father, may give you the Spirit of
wisdom and revelation, so that you
may know Him better. I pray also
that the eyes of your heart may
be enlightened in order that you
may know the hope to which He
has called you, the riches of His
glorious inheritance in the saints,
and His incomparably great power
for us who believe. That power
is like the working of His mighty
strength, which He exerted in Christ
when He raised Him from the dead
and seated Him at His right hand
in the heavenly realms, far above
all rule and authority, power and
dominion, and every title that can
be given, not only in the present
age but also in the one to come.

CONFESSING *God's Word*

And God placed all things under His feet and appointed Him to be head over everything for the church, which is His body, the fullness of Him who fills everything in every way. (Eph. 1:17-23)

❧

And this is my prayer: That your love may abound more and more in knowledge and depth of insight, so that you may be able to discern what is best and may be pure and blameless until the day of Christ, filled with the fruit of righteousness that comes through Jesus Christ—to the glory and praise of God. (Phil.1:9-11)

❧

We have not stopped praying for you and asking God to fill you with the knowledge of His will through all spiritual wisdom and understanding. And we pray this in order that you may live a life worthy of the Lord and may please Him in every way, bearing fruit in every good work, growing in the knowledge of God, being strengthened with all power—according to His glorious might so that you may have great endurance and patience, and joyfully giving thanks to the Father, Who has qualified you to share in the inheritance of the saints in the kingdom of light. For He has rescued us from the dominion of darkness and brought us into the kingdom of the Son He loves, in whom we have redemption, the forgiveness of sins. (Col. 1:9-14)

CONFESSING *God's Word*

That the communication of thy faith may become effectual by the acknowledging of every good thing which is in you in Christ Jesus. (Philemon 6 KJV)

Chapter Thirteen

Scriptures for
Husbands
to Pray

Confessing *God's Word*

My wife is a suitable helper for me. (Gen. 2:18)

❧

I have full confidence in my wife and lack nothing of value. (Prov. 31:11)

❧

My wife brings me good, not harm, all the days of her life. (Prov. 31:12)

❧

My wife watches over the affairs of my household, and she does not eat the bread of idleness. (Prov. 31:27)

❧

My wife is of noble character, and she is worth far more than rubies to me. (Prov. 31:10)

146

SCRIPTURES FOR HUSBANDS

I am considerate as I live with my wife, and I treat her with respect as the weaker partner and as heir with me of the gracious gift of life, so that nothing will hinder my prayers. (1 Pet. 3:7)

❦

I have found what is good, and I have received favor from the Lord, for I have found my wife. (Prov. 18:22)

❦

...my wife excels them all...for my wife reverently and worshipfully fears the Lord, and she shall be praised. (Prov. 31:29, 30)

❦

My wife is a fruitful vine within my house; and my sons are like olive shoots around my table. (Ps. 128:3)

CONFESSING *God's Word*

I love my wife, and I am not harsh with her. (Col. 3:19)

❧

My wife is the workmanship of God, created in Christ Jesus to do good works, which God prepared in advance for her to do. (Eph. 2:10)

148

CHAPTER FOURTEEN

Scriptures for
WIVES
to Pray

Confessing *God's Word*

My husband submits himself to God. He resists the devil, and the devil flees from him. My husband draws near to God, and God draws near to him. (James 4:7)

❧

My husband is wise and understanding. He shows it by his good life and by deeds done in the humility that comes from wisdom. (James 3:13)

❧

My husband's steps are directed by the Lord. (Prov. 20:24)

❧

My husband gives heed to instruction so he prospers, and he is blessed because he trusts in the Lord. (Prov. 16:20)

Scriptures for Wives

My husband is strong in the Lord and His mighty power. (Eph. 6:10)

~

My husband's faith does not rest on men's wisdom but on God's power. (1 Cor. 2:5)

~

My husband gives gentle answers which turn away wrath. (Prov. 15:1)

~

My husband trusts in the Lord with all his heart and leans not on his own understanding. In all his ways he acknowledges God, and God makes his path straight. (Prov. 3:5-6)

~

My husband loves me as his own body. (Eph. 5:28)

My generous husband will prosper; and while he refreshes others, he himself will be refreshed. (Prov. 11:25)

❧

My husband obeys and serves God, and we will spend the rest of our days in prosperity and our years in contentment. (Job 36:11)

❧

I am a wise woman; I build my house. (Prov. 14:1)

❧

I love my husband and children, I am self-controlled and pure, I am busy at home, I am kind, and subject to my husband so that no one will malign the Word of God. (Titus 2:4-5)

Scriptures for Wives

I submit to my husband as is fitting in the Lord. (Col. 3:18)

⸎

I am a wife of noble character and I am a crown to my husband. (Prov. 12:4)

⸎

My husband loves me, just as Christ loved the church and gave himself up for her. (Eph. 5:25)

⸎

I am bound to my husband as long as he lives. (1 Cor. 7:39a)

⸎

My husband is God's workmanship, created in Christ Jesus to do good works, which God prepared in advance for him to do. (Eph. 2:10)

CONFESSING *God's Word*

I watch over the affairs of my household, and I do not eat the bread of idleness. (Prov. 31:27)

Through Christ Jesus the law of the Spirit of life has set my husband free from the law of sin and death. (Rom. 8:2)

I bring my husband good and not harm, all the days of my life. (Prov. 31:12)

My husband loves me as he loves himself, and I respect him. (Eph. 5:33)

My husband loves me and is not harsh with me. (Col. 3:19)

SCRIPTURE TOPICS

CONFESSING *God's Word*

CHAPTER FIFTEEN

FAITH
Scriptures

Confessing *God's Word*

Be strong and courageous. Do not be afraid or discouraged because of the king of Assyria and the vast army with him, for there is a greater power with us than with him. (2 Chron. 32:7)

~

Now give me this hill country that the Lord promised me. You yourself heard that the Anakites were there and their cities were large and fortified, but, the Lord helping me, I will drive them out just as He said. (Josh. 14:12)

~

However, to the man who does not work but trusts God who justifies the wicked, his faith is credited as righteousness. (Rom. 4:5)

Faith Scriptures

This righteousness from God comes through faith in Jesus Christ to all who believe. (Rom. 3:22)

⚜

For if those who live by law are heirs, faith has no value and the promise is worthless, because law brings wrath. (Rom. 4:14-15)

⚜

So keep up your courage, men, for I have faith in God that it will happen just as He told me. (Acts 27:25)

⚜

What then shall we say? That the Gentiles, who did not pursue righteousness, have obtained it, a righteousness that is by faith. (Rom. 9:30)

CONFESSING *God's Word*

Abram believed the Lord, and God credited it to him as righteousness. (Gen. 15:6)

❧

Our enemy is only the arm of the flesh, but with us is the Lord our God to help us and to fight our battles. (2 Chron. 32:8)

❧

The Lord who delivered me from the paw of the lion and the paw of the bear will deliver me from the hand of this Philistine. (1 Sam. 17:37)

❧

First, I thank my God through Jesus Christ for all of you, because your faith is being reported all over the world. (Rom. 1:8)

160

FAITH SCRIPTURES

We have been saying that Abraham's faith was credited to him as righteousness. (Rom. 4:9b)

❧

See, he is puffed up; his desires are not upright—but the righteous will live by his faith. (Hab. 2:4)

❧

We walk in the footsteps of the faith that our father, Abraham, had before he was circumcised. (Rom. 4:12)

❧

It was not through law that Abraham and his offspring received the promise that he would be heir of the world, but through the righteousness that comes by faith. (Rom. 4:13)

CONFESSING *God's Word*

Through Him and for His name's sake, we received grace and apostleship to call people from among all the Gentiles to the obedience that comes from faith. (Rom. 1:5)

❧

For in the Gospel a righteousness from God is revealed, a righteousness that is by faith from first to last, just as it is written, "The righteous will live by faith." (Rom. 1:17)

❧

And he received the sign of circumcision, a seal of the righteousness that he had by faith while he was still uncircumcised. (Rom. 4:11)

Faith Scriptures

Therefore, the promise comes by faith, so that it may be by grace and may be guaranteed to all Abraham's offspring. (Rom. 4:16)

❧

Without weakening in his faith, he faced the fact that his body was as good as dead since he was about a hundred years old and that Sarah's womb was also dead. (Rom. 4:19)

❧

Yet he did not waver through unbelief regarding the promise of God, but was strengthened in his faith and gave glory to God, being fully persuaded that God had power to do what He had promised. (Rom. 4:20, 21)

CONFESSING *God's Word*

Therefore, since we have been justified through faith, we have peace with God through our Lord Jesus Christ, through whom we have gained access by faith into this grace in which we now stand. (Rom. 5:1-2)

❧

For it is by grace you have been saved, through faith—and this not from yourselves, it is the gift of God. (Eph. 2:8)

❧

By faith Abraham, even though he was past age—and Sarah herself was barren—was enabled to become a father because he considered Him faithful who had made the promise. (Heb. 11:11)

FAITH SCRIPTURES

And without faith it is impossible to please God, because anyone who comes to Him must believe that He exists and that He rewards those who earnestly seek Him. (Heb. 11:6)

❧

Trust in the Lord with all your heart and lean not on you own understanding; in all your ways acknowledge Him, and He will direct your path. (Prov. 3:5, 6 KJV)

❧

The Lord said, "If as one people speaking the same language they have begun to do this, then nothing they plan to do will be impossible for them." (Gen. 11:6)

CONFESSING *God's Word*

Now faith is being sure of what we hope for and certain of what we do not see. (Heb. 11:1)

❧

For in Christ Jesus neither circumcision nor uncircumcision has any value. The only thing that counts is faith expressing itself through love. (Gal. 5:6)

❧

So then faith comes by hearing, and hearing by the Word of God. (Rom. 10:17 NKJV)

❧

By faith we understand that the universe was formed at God's command, so that what is seen was not made out of what was visible. (Heb. 11:3)

Faith Scriptures

Those, who went before us, through faith conquered kingdoms, administered justice, and gained what was promised; who shut the mouths of lions, quenched the fury of the flames, and escaped the edge of the sword; whose weakness was turned to strength; and who became powerful in battle and routed foreign armies. (Heb. 11:33, 34)

For we also have had the Gospel preached to us, just as they did; but the message they heard was of no value to them, because those who heard did not combine it with faith. Now we who have believed enter that rest. (Heb. 4:2, 3a)

CONFESSING *God's Word*

So we fix our eyes not on what is seen, but on what is unseen. For what is seen is temporary, but what is unseen is eternal. (2 Cor. 4:18)

❧

"Have faith in God," Jesus answered, "I tell you the truth, if anyone says to this mountain, 'Go, throw yourself into the sea,' and does not doubt in his heart but believes that what he says will happen, it will be done for him. Therefore I tell you, whatever you ask for in prayer, believe that you have received it, and it will be yours." (Mark 11:22-24)

❧

Everything is possible for him who believes. (Mark 9:23)

FAITH SCRIPTURES

He replied, "Because you have so little faith. I tell you the truth, if you have faith as small as a mustard seed, you can say to this mountain, 'Move from here to there' and it will move. Nothing will be impossible for you." (Matt. 17:20)

❧

God presented Him as a sacrifice of atonement, through faith in His blood. He did this to demonstrate His justice, because in His forbearance He had left the sins committed beforehand unpunished—He did it to demonstrate His justice at the present time, so as to be just and the One who justifies those who have faith in Jesus. (Rom. 3:25-26)

Where, then, is boasting?—It is excluded. On what principle? On that of observing the law? No, but on that of faith. For we maintain that a man is justified by faith apart from observing the law. (Rom. 3:25-28)

❧

That the communication of your faith may become effectual by the acknowledging of every good thing which is in you in Christ Jesus. (Philemon 6 KJV)

❧

By faith Abraham, when called to go to a place he would later receive as his inheritance, obeyed and went, even though he did not know where he was going. (Heb. 11:8)

FAITH SCRIPTURES

But you, dear friends, build yourselves up in Your most holy faith, and pray in the Holy Spirit. (Jude 20)

Confessing *God's Word*

CH

CONFESSING

I am the most
my lips have
since God
45:2)

GRACE
Scriptures

excellent of men and
been anointed with grace,
has blessed me forever. (Ps.

❧

preserve sound judgment and
discernment; I do not let them out
of my sight; they will be life for me,
an ornament to grace my neck. (Prov.
3:21, 22)

❧

And the child grew and became
strong; he was filled with wisdom,
and the grace of God was upon him.
(Luke 2:40)

❧

Those who cling to worthless idols
forfeit the grace that could be theirs.
(Jonah 2:8)

174

GRACE SCRIPTURES

Listen, my son, to your father's instruction and do not forsake your mother's teaching. They will be a garland to grace your head and a chain to adorn your neck. (Prov. 1:8, 9)

❧

He mocks proud mockers but gives grace to the humble. (Prov. 3:34)

❧

And I will pour out on the house of David and the inhabitants of Jerusalem a spirit of grace and supplication. (Zech. 12:10a)

❧

We have seen His glory, the glory of the One and Only, who came from the Father, full of grace and truth. (John 1:14)

Confessing *God's Word*

With great power the apostles continued to testify to the resurrection of the Lord Jesus, and much grace was upon them all. (Acts 4:33)

❧

When he arrived and saw the evidence of the grace of God, he was glad and encouraged them all to remain true to the Lord with all their hearts. (Acts 11:23)

❧

From the fullness of His grace I have received one blessing after another. (John 1:16)

❧

For the law was given through Moses; grace and truth came through Jesus Christ. (John 1:17)

Now Stephen, a man full of God's grace and power, did great wonders and miraculous signs among the people. (Acts 6:8)

❧

I have gained access by faith into this grace in which I now stand. (Rom. 5:2)

❧

Through Him and for His name's sake, I received grace and apostleship to call people from among all the Gentiles to the obedience that comes from faith. (Rom. 1:5)

❧

Grace and peace to you from God our Father and from the Lord Jesus Christ. (Rom. 1:7b)

And all are justified freely by His grace through the redemption that came by Christ Jesus. (Rom. 3:24)

❧

Therefore, the promise comes by faith, so that it may be by grace and may be guaranteed to all Abraham's offspring. (Rom. 4:16a)

❧

Those who receive God's abundant provision of grace and of the gift of righteousness reign in life through the one man, Jesus Christ. (Rom. 5:17b)

❧

For sin shall not be my master, because I am not under law, but under grace. (Rom. 6:14)

GRACE SCRIPTURES

God's grace and the gift that came by the grace of the one man, Jesus Christ, overflow to the many! (Rom. 5:15b)

❧

Grace might reign through righteousness to bring eternal life through Jesus Christ our Lord. (Rom. 5:21b)

❧

Grace from God was given me to be a minister of Christ Jesus. (Rom. 15:15b)

❧

And God is able to make all grace abound to me, so that in all things at all times, having all that I need, I will abound in every good work. (2 Cor. 9:8)

CONFESSING *God's Word*

And if by grace, then it is no longer by works; if it were, grace would no longer be grace. (Rom. 11:6)

❧

For I know the grace of our Lord Jesus Christ, that though He was rich, yet for my sake He became poor, so that I through His poverty might become rich. (2 Cor. 8:9)

❧

I always thank God for you because of His grace given you in Christ Jesus. (1 Cor. 1:4)

❧

I do not set aside the grace of God, for if righteousness could be gained through the law, Christ died for nothing! (Gal. 2:21)

GRACE SCRIPTURES

But by the grace of God I am what I am, and His grace to me was not without effect. No, I worked harder than all of them—yet not I, but the grace of God that was with me. (1 Cor. 15:10)

It is good for my heart to be strengthened by grace. (Heb. 13:9b)

God, who set me apart from birth and called me by His grace. (Gal. 1:15)

The grace of our Lord was poured out on me abundantly, along with the faith and love that are in Christ Jesus. (1 Tim. 1:14)

CONFESSING *God's Word*

I approach the throne of grace with confidence, so that I may receive mercy and find grace to help me in my time of need. (Heb. 4:16)

❧

For the grace of God that brings salvation has appeared to me. It teaches me to say, "No," to ungodliness and worldly passions, and to live a self-controlled, upright and godly life in this present age. (Titus 2:11-12)

❧

We have different gifts, according to the grace given us. If a man's gift is prophesying, let him use it in proportion to his faith. (Rom. 12:6)

GRACE SCRIPTURES

Surely you have heard about the administration of God's grace that was given to me for you. (Eph. 3:2)

❧

For it is by grace I have been saved, through faith—and this not from myself; it is the gift of God— not by works, so that no one can boast. (Eph. 2:8-9)

❧

Although I am less than the least of all God's people, this grace was given me to preach to the Gentiles the unsearchable riches of Christ, and to make plain to everyone the administration of this mystery, which for ages past was kept hidden in God, who created all things. (Eph. 3:8-9)

CONFESSING *God's Word*

I see to it that I do not miss the grace of God and that no bitter root grows up to cause trouble and defile many. (Heb. 12:15)

~

For if the inheritance depends on the law, then it no longer depends on a promise; but God in His grace gave it to Abraham through a promise. (Gal. 3:18)

~

They are godless men, who change the grace of our God into a license for immorality and deny Jesus Christ our only Sovereign and Lord. (Jude 4b)

~

God opposes the proud but gives grace to the humble. (James 4:6b)

184

Grace Scriptures

By the grace God has given me, I laid a foundation as an expert builder. (1 Cor. 3:10a)

❧

I always let my conversation be full of grace, seasoned with salt, so that I may know how to answer everyone. (Col. 4:6)

❧

May our Lord Jesus Christ himself and God our Father, who loved me and by His grace gave me eternal encouragement and good hope. (2 Thes. 2:16)

❧

I became a servant of this Gospel by the gift of God's grace given me through the working of His power. (Eph. 3:7)

Confessing *God's Word*

In Him I have redemption through His blood, the forgiveness of sins, in accordance with the riches of God's grace that He lavished on me with all wisdom and understanding. (Eph. 1:7-8)

⸙

You who are trying to be justified by law have been alienated from Christ; you have fallen away from grace. (Gal. 5:4)

⸙

But to each one of us grace has been given as Christ apportioned it. (Eph. 4:7)

⸙

My grace is sufficient for you, for my power is made perfect in weakness. (2 Cor. 12:9a)

186

CHAPTER SEVENTEEN

JOY
Scriptures

Confessing *God's Word*

Blessed am I when men hate me, when they exclude me and insult me and reject my name as evil, because of the Son of Man. I rejoice in that day and leap for joy, because great is my reward in heaven. (Luke 6:22-23a)

❧

...at His tabernacle will I sacrifice with shouts of joy; I will sing and make music to the Lord. (Ps. 27:6b)

❧

For the kingdom of God is...of righteousness, peace, and joy in the Holy Spirit, because anyone who serves Christ in this way is pleasing to God and approved by men. (Rom. 14:17-18)

JOY SCRIPTURES

My heart leaps for joy, and I will give thanks to Him in song. (Ps. 28:7b)

❧

Clap your hands, all you nations; shout to God with cries of joy. (Ps. 47:1)

❧

Restore to me the joy of your salvation and grant me a willing spirit to sustain me. (Ps. 51:12)

❧

Then will I go to the altar of God, to God, my joy and my delight. (Ps. 43:4a)

❧

You have made known to me the paths of life; You will fill me with joy in Your presence. (Acts 2:28)

CONFESSING *God's Word*

...made him glad with the joy of Your presence. (Ps. 21:6b)

❧

I have told you this so that My joy may be in you and that your joy may be complete. (John 15:11)

❧

Ask and you will receive, and your joy will be complete. (John 16:24b)

❧

And the disciples were filled with joy and with the Holy Spirit. (Acts 13:52)

❧

...in spite of severe suffering, you welcomed the message with the joy given by the Holy Spirit. (1 Thes. 1:6b)

190

...is full of joy when he hears the bridegroom's voice. (John 3:29b)

❧

I do not grieve, for the joy of the Lord is my strength. (Neh. 8:10b)

❧

May the God of hope fill me with all joy and peace as I trust in Him... (Rom. 15:13a)

❧

...so that I may have the full measure of Your joy within me. (John 17:13b)

❧

I have loved righteousness and hated wickedness; therefore God, my God, has set me above my companions by anointing me with the oil of joy. (Heb. 1:9)

CONFESSING *God's Word*

...I love Him...I believe in Him and I am filled with an inexpressible and glorious joy, for I am receiving the goal of my faith, the salvation of my soul. (1 Pet. 1:8, 9)

❧

I obey my leaders...so that my work will be a joy, not a burden... (Heb. 13:17)

❧

I consider it pure joy, my brothers, whenever I face trials of many kinds... (James 1:2)

❧

And our fellowship is with the Father and with His Son, Jesus Christ. We write this to make our joy complete. (1 John 1:3b, 4)

❧

I am joyful always; I pray continually... (1 Thes. 5:16, 17)

192

Read the
BIBLE
in a Year

CONFESSING *God's Word*

1 Gen 1:1-2:25, Matt 1:1-2:12, Ps 1:1-6, Prov 1:1-6

2 Gen 3:1-4:26, Matt 2:13-3:6, Ps 2:1-12, Prov 1:7-9

3 Gen 5:1-7:24, Matt 3:7-4:11, Ps 3:1-8, Prov 1:10-19

4 Gen 8:1-10:32, Matt 4:12-25, Ps 4:1-8, Prov 1:20-23

5 Gen 11:1-13:4, Matt 5:1-26, Ps 5:1-12, Prov 1:24-28

6 Gen 13:5-15:21, Matt 5:27-48, Ps 6:1-10, Prov 1:29-33

7 Gen 16:1-18:19, Matt 6:1-24, Ps 7:1-17, Prov 2:1-5

8 Gen 18:20-19:38, Matt 6:25-7:14, Ps 8:1-9, Prov 2:6-15

9 Gen 20:1-22:24, Matt 7:15-29, Ps 9:1-12, Prov 2:16-22

10 Gen 23:1-24:51, Matt 8:1-17, Ps 9:13-20, Prov 3:1-6

11 Gen 24:52-26:16, Matt 8:18-34, Ps 10:1-15, Prov 3:7-8

12 Gen 26:17-27:46, Matt 9:1-17, Ps 10:16-18, Prov 3:9-10

13 Gen 28:1-29:35, Matt 9:18-38, Ps 11:1-7, Prov 3:11-12

14 Gen 30:1-31:16, Matt 10:1-25, Ps 12:1-8, Prov 3:13-15

15 Gen 31:17-32:12, Matt 10:26-11:6, Ps 13:1-6, Prov 3:16-18

16 Gen 32:13-34:31, Matt 11:7-30, Ps 14:1-7, Prov 3:19-30

194

January

17 Gen 35:1-36:43, Matt 12:1-21, Ps 15:1-5, Prov 3:21-26

18 Gen 37:1-38:30, Matt 12:22-45, Ps 16:1-11, Prov 3:27-32

19 Gen 39:1-41:16, Matt 12:46-13:23, Ps 17:1-15, Prov 3:33-35

20 Gen 41:17-42:17, Matt 13:24-46, Ps 18:1-15, Prov 4:1-6

21 Gen 42:18-43:34, Matt 13:47-14:12, Ps 18:16-36, Prov 4:7-10

22 Gen 44:1-45:28, Matt 14:13-36, Ps 18:37-50, Prov 4:11-13

23 Gen 46:1-47:31, Matt 15:1-28, Ps 19:1-14, Prov 4:14-19

24 Gen 48:1-49:33, Matt 15:29-16:12, Ps 20:1-9, Prov 4:20-27

25 Gen 50:1- Ex 2:10, Matt 16:13-17:9, Ps 21:1-3, Prov 5:1-6

26 Ex 2:11-3:22, Matt 17:10-27, Ps 22:1-18, Prov 5:7-14

27 Ex 4:1-5:21, Matt 18:1-22, Ps 22:19-31, Prov 5:15-21

28 Ex 5:22-7:24, Matt 18:23-19:12, Ps 23:1-6, Prov 5:22-23

29 Ex 7:25-9:35, Matt 19:13-30, Ps 24:1-10, Prov 6:1-5

30 Ex 10:1-12:13, Matt 20:1-28, Ps 25:1-15, Prov 6:6-11

31 Ex 12:14-13:16, Matt 20:29-21:22, Ps 25:16-22, Prov 6:12-15

Confessing *God's Word*

1 Ex 13:17-15:18, Matt 21:23-46, Ps 26:1-12, Prov 6:16-19

2 Ex 15:19-17:7, Matt 22:1-33, Ps 27:1-6, Prov 6:20-26

3 Ex 17:8-19:15, Matt 22:34-23:12, Ps 27:7-14, Prov 6:27-35

4 Ex 19:16-21:21, Matt 23:13-39, Ps 28:1-9, Prov 7:1-5

5 Ex 21:22-23:13, Matt 24:1-28, Ps 29:1-11, Prov 7:6-23

6 Ex 23:14-25:40, Matt 24:29-51, Ps 30:1-12, Prov 7:24-27

7 Ex 26:1-27:21, Matt 25:1-30, Ps 31:1-8, Prov 8:1-11

8 Ex 28:1-43, Matt 25:31-26:13, Ps 31:9-18, Prov 8:12-13

9 Ex 29:1-30:10, Matt 26:14-46, Ps 31:19-24, Prov 8:14-26

10 Ex 30:11-31:18, Matt 26:46-68, Ps 32:1-11, Prov 8:27-32

11 Ex 32:1-33:23, Matt 26:69-27:14, Ps 33:1-11, Prov 8:33-36

12 Ex 34:1-35:9, Matt 27:15-31, Ps 33:12-22, Prov 9:1-6

13 Ex 35:10-36:38, Matt 27:32-66, Ps 34:1-10, Prov 9:7-8

14 Ex 37:1-38:31, Matt 28:1-20, Ps 34:11-22, Prov 9:9-10

15 Ex 39:1-40:38, Mk 1:1-28, Ps 35:1-16, Prov 9:11-12

16 Lev 1:1-3:17, Mk 1:29-2:12, Ps 35:17-28, Prov 13:13-18

February

17 Lev 4:1-5:19, Mk 2:13-3:6, Ps 36:1-12, Prov 10:1-2

18 Lev 6:1-7:27, Mk 3:7-30, Ps 37:1-11, Prov 10:3-4

19 Lev 7:28-9:6, Mk 3:31-4:25, Ps 37:12-29, Prov 10:5

20 Lev 9:7-10:20, Mk 4:26-5:20, Ps 37:30-40, Prov 10:6-7

21 Lev 11:1-12:8, Mk 5:21-43, Ps 38:1-22, Prov 10:8-9

22 Lev 13:1-59, Mk 6:1-29, Ps 39:1-13, Prov 10:10

23 Lev 14:1-57, Mk 6:30-56, Ps 40:1-10, Prov 10:11-12

24 Lev 15:1-16:28, Mk 7:1-23, Ps 40:11-17, Prov 10:13-14

25 Lev 16:29-29-18:30, Mk 7:24-8:10, Ps 41:1-13, Prov 10:15-16

26 Lev 149:1-20:21, Mk 8:11-38, Ps 42:1-11, Prov 10:17

27 Lev 20:22-22:16, Mk 9:1-29, Ps 43:1-5, Prov 10:18

28 Lev 22:17-23:44, Mk 9:30-10:12, Ps 44:1-8, Prov 10:19, 6:12-15

197

Confessing *God's Word*

1   Lev 24:1-25:46, Mk 10:13-31, Ps 44:9-26, Prov 10:20-21

2   Lev 25:47-27:13, Mk 10:32-52, Ps 45:1-17, Prov 10:22

3   Lev 27:14-Num 1:54, Mk 11:1-25, Ps 46:1-11, Prov 10:23

4   Num 2:1-3:51, Mk 11:27-12:17, Ps 47:1-9, Prov 10:24-25

5   Num 4:1-5:31, Mk 12:18-37, Ps 48:1-14, Prov 10:26

6   Num 6:1-7:89, Mk 12:38-13:13, Ps 49:1-20, Prov 10:27-28

7   Num 8:1-9:23, Mk 13:14-37, Ps 50:1-23, Prov 10:29-30

8   Num 10:1-11:23, Mk 14:1-21, Ps 51:1-19, Prov 10:31-32

9   Num 11:24-13:33, Mk 14:22-52, Ps 52:1-9, Prov 11:1-3

10   Num 14:1-15:16, Mk 14:53-72, Ps 53:1-6, Prov 11:4

11   Num 15:17-16:40, Mk 15:1-47, Ps 54:1-7, Prov 11:5-6

12   Num 16:41-18:32, Mk 16:1-20, Ps 55:1-23, Prov 11:7

13   Num 19:1-20:29, Lk 1:1-25, Ps 56:1-13, Prov 11:8

14   Num 21:1-22:20, Lk 1:26-56, Ps 57:1-11, Prov 11:9-11

15   Num 22:21-23:30, Lk 1:57-80, Ps 58:1-11, Prov 11:12-13

16   Num 24:1-25:18, Lk 2:1-35, Ps 59:1-17, Prov 11:14

MARCH

17 Num 26:1-51, Lk 2:36-52, Ps 60:1-12, Prov 11:15

18 Num 26:52-28:15, Lk 3:1-22, Ps 61:1-8, Prov 11:16-17

19 Num 28:16-29:40, Lk 3:23-38, Ps 62:1-12, Prov 11:18-19

20 Num 30:1-31:54, Lk 4:1-30, Ps 63:1-11, Prov 11:20-21

21 Num 32:1-33:39, Lk 4:31-5:11, Ps 64:1-10, Prov 11:22

22 Num 33:40-35:34, Lk 5:12-28, Ps 65:1-13, Prov 11:23

23 Num 36:1-Dt 1:46, Lk 5:29-6:11, Ps 66:1-20, Prov 11:24-26

24 Dt 2:1-3:29, Lk 6:12-38, Ps 67:1-7, Prov 11:27

25 Dt 4:1-49, Lk 6:39-7:10, Ps 68:1-18, Prov 11:28

26 Dt 5:1-6:25, Lk 7:11-35, Ps 68:19-35, Prov 11:29-31

27 Dt 7:1-8:20, Lk 7:36-8:3, Ps 69:1-18, Prov 12:1

28 Dt 9:1-10:22, Lk 8:4-21, Ps 69:19:36, Prov 12:2-3

29 Dt 11:1-12:32, Lk 8:22-39, Ps 70:1-5, Prov 12:4

30 Dt 13:1-15:23, Lk 8:40-9:6, Ps 71:1-24, Prov 12:5-7

31 Dt 16:1-17:20, Lk 9:7-27, Ps 72:1-20, Prov 12:8-9

CONFESSING *God's Word*

1 Dt 18:1-20:20, Lk 9:28-50, Ps 73:1-28, Prov 12:10

2 Dt 21:1-22:30, Lk 9:51-10:12, Ps 74:1-23, Prov 12:11

3 Dt 23:1-25:19, Lk 10:13-37, Ps 75:1-10, Prov 12:12-14

4 Dt 26:1-27:26, Lk 10:38-11:13, Ps 76:1-12, Prov 12:15-17

5 Dt 28:1-68, Lk 11:14-36, Ps 77:1-20, Prov 12:18

6 Dt 29:1-30:20, Lk 11:37-12:7, Ps 78:1-31, Prov 12:19-20

7 Dt 31:1-32:27, Lk 12:8-34, Ps 78:32-55, Prov 12:21-23

8 Dt 32:28-52, Lk 12:35-59, Ps 78:56-64, Prov 12:24

9 Dt 33:1-29, Lk 13:1-21, Ps 78:65-72, Prov 12:25

10 Dt 34:1-Josh 2:24, Lk 13:22-14:6, Ps 79:1-13, Prov 12:26

11 Josh 3:1-4:24, Lk 14:7-35, Ps 80:1-19, Prv 12:27-28

12 Josh 5:1-7:15, Lk 15:1-32, Ps 81:1-16, Prov 13:1

13 Josh 7:16-9:2, Lk 16:1-18, Ps 82:1-8, Prov 13:2-3

14 Josh 9:3-10:43, Lk 16:19-17:10, Ps 83:1-18, Prov 13:4

15 Josh 11:1-12:24, Lk 17:11-37, Ps 84:1-12, Prov 13:5-6

16 Josh 13:1-14:15, Lk 18:1-17, Ps 85:1-13, Prov 13:7-8

APRIL

CONFESSING *God's Word*

1 Jdg 13:1-14:20, Jn 1:29-51, Ps 102:1-28, Prov 14:15-16

2 Jdg 15:1-16:31, Jn 2:1-25, Ps 103:1-22, Prov 14:17-19

3 Jdg 17:1-18:31, Jn 3:1-21, Ps 104:1-23, Prov 14:20-21

4 Jdg 19:1-20:48, Jn 3:22-4:3, Ps 104:24-35, Prov 14:22-24

5 Jdg 21:1-Rth 1:22, Jn 4:4-42, Ps 105:1-15, Prov 14:25

6 Rth 2:1-4:22, Jn 4:43-54, Ps 105:16-36, Prov 14:26-27

7 1 Sam 1:1-2:21, Jn 5:1-23, Ps 105:37-45, Prov 14:28-29

8 1 Sam 2:22-4:22, Jn 5:24-47, Ps 106:1-12, Prov 14:30-31

9 1 Sam 5:1-7:17, Jn 6:1-21, Ps 106:13-31, Prov 14:32-33

10 1 Sam 8:1-9:27, Jn 6:22-42, Ps 106:32-48, Prov 14:34-35

11 1 Sam 10:1-11:15, Jn 6:43-71, Ps 107:1-43, Prov 15:1-3

12 1 Sam 12:1-13:22, Jn 7:1-29, Ps 108:1-13, Prov 15:4

13 1 Sam 13:23-14:52, Jn 7:30-53, Ps 109:1-31, Prov 15:5-7

14 1 Sam 15:1-16:23, Jn 8:1-12, Ps 110:1-7, Prov 15:8-10

15 1 Sam 17:1-18:4, Jn 8:21-30, Ps 11:1-10, Prov 15:11

16 1 Sam 18:5-19:24, Jn 8:31-59, Ps 112:1-10, Prov 15:12-14

May

17 1 Sam 20:1-21:15, Jn 9:1-41, Ps 113:1-114:8, Prov 15:15-17

18 1 Sam 22:1-23:29, Jn 10:1-21, Ps 115:1-18, Prov 15:18-19

19 1 Sam 24:1-25:44, Jn 10:22-42, Ps 116:1-19, Prov 15:20-21

20 1 Sam 26:1-28:25, Jn 11:1-53, Ps 117:1-2, Prov 15:22-23

21 1 Sam 29:1-31:13, Jn 11:54-12:19, Ps 118:1-18, Prov 15:24-26

22 2 Sam 1:1-2:11, Jn 12:20-50, Ps 118:19-29, Prov 15:27-28

23 2 Sam 2:12-3:39, Jn 13:1-30, Ps 119:1-16, Prov 15:29-30

24 2 Sam 4:1-6:23, Jn 13:31-14:14, Ps 119:17-32, Prov 15:31-32

25 2 Sam 7:1-8:18, Jn 14:15-31, Ps 119:33-48, Prov 15:33

26 2 Sam 9:1-11:27, Jn 15:1-27, Ps 119:49-64, Prov 16:1-3

27 2 Sam 12:1-31, Km 16:1-33, Ps 119:65-80, Prov 16:4-5

28 2 Sam 13:1-39, Jn 17:1-26, Ps 119:81-96, Prov 16:6-7

29 2 Sam 14:1-15:22. Jn 18:1-24, Ps 119:97-112, Prov 16:8-9

30 2 Sam 15:23-16:23, Jn 18:25-19:22, Ps 119:113-128, Prov 15:10-11

31 2 Sam 17:1-29, Jn 19:23-42, Ps 119:129-152, Prov 16:12-13

Confessing *God's Word*

JUNE

Confessing *God's Word*

1 2 Kgs 18:13-19:37, Act 21:1-16, Ps 149:1-9, Prov 18:8

2 2 Kgs 20:1-22:2, Act 21:17-36, Ps 150:1-6, Prov 18:9-10

3 2 Kgs 22:3-23:30, Act 21:37-22:16, Ps 1:1-6, Prov 18:11-12

4 2 Kgs 23:31-25:30, Act 22:17-23:10, Ps 2:1-12, Prov 18:13

5 1 Chr 1:1-2:17, Act 23:11-35, Ps 3:1-8, Prov 18:14-15

6 1 Chr 2:18-4:4, Act 24:1-27, Ps 4:1-8, Prov 18:16-18

7 1 Chr 4:5-5:17, Act 25:1-27, Ps 5:1-12, Prov 18:19

8 1 Chr 5:18-6:81, Act 26:1-32, Ps 6:1-10, Prov 18:20-21

9 1 Chr 7:1-8:40. Act 27:1-20, Ps 7:1-17, Prov 18:22

10 1 Chr 9:1-10:14, Act 27:21-44, Ps 8:1-9:20, Prov 18:23-24

11 1 Chr 11:1-12:18, Act 28:1-31, Ps 9:1-12, Prov 19:1-3

12 1 Chr 12:19-14:17, Rom 1:1-17, Ps 9:13-20, Prov 19:4-5

13 1 Chr 15:1-16:36, Rom 1:18-32, Ps 10:1-15, Prov 19:6-7

14 1 Chr 16:37-18:17, Rom, 2:1-24, Ps 10:16-18, Prov 19:8-9

15 1 Chr 19:1-21:30, Rom, 2:25-3:8, Ps 11:1-7, Prov 19:10-12

16 1 Chr 22:1-23:32, Rom 3:9-31, Ps 12:1-8, Prov 19:13-14

JULY

17 1 Chr 24:1-26:11, Rom 4:1-2, Ps 13:1-6, Prov 19:15-16

18 1 Chr 26:12-27:34, Rom 4:13-5:5, Ps 14:1-7, Prov 19:17

19 1 Chr 28:1-29:30, Rom 5:6-21, Ps 15:1-5, Prov 19:18-19

20 2 Chr 1:1-3:17, Rom 6:1-23, Ps 16:1-11, Prov 19:20-21

21 2 Chr 4:1-6:11, Rom 7:1-13, Ps 17:1-15, Prov 19:22-23

22 2 Chr 6:12-8:10, Rom 7:14-8:8, Ps 18:1-15, Prov 19:24-25

23 2 Chr 8:11-10:19, Rom 8:9-21, Ps 18:16-36, Prov 19:26

24 2 Chr 11:1-13:22, Rom 8:22-39, Ps 18:37-50, Prov 19:27-29

25 2 Chr 14:1-16:14, Rom 9:1-21, Ps 19:1-14, Prov 20:1

26 2 Chr 17:1-18:34, Rom 9:22-10:13, Ps 20:1-9, Prov 20:2-3

27 2 Chr 19:1-20:37, Rom 10:14-11:12, Ps 21:1-13, Prov 20:4-6

28 2 Chr 21:1-23:21, Rom 11:13-36, Ps 22:1-18, Prov 20:7

29 2 Chr 24:1-25:28, Rom 12:1-21, Ps 22:19-31, Prov 20:8-10

30 2 Chr 26:1-28:27, Rom 13:1-14, Ps 23:1-6, Prov 20:11

31 2 Chr 29:1-36, Rom 14:1-23, Ps 24:1-10, Prov 20:12

Confessing *God's Word*

1   2 Chr 30:1-31:21, Rom 15:1-22, Ps 25:1-5, Prov 20:13-15

2   2 Chr 32:1-33:13, Rom 15:23-16:7, Ps 25:16-22, Prov 20:16-18

3   2 Chr 33:14-34:33, Rom 16:8-27, Ps 26:1-12, Prov 20:19

4   2 Chr 25:1-36:23, 1 Cor 1:1-17, Ps 27:1-6, Prov 20:20-21

5   Ezr 1:1-2:70, 1 Cor 1:18-2:5, Ps 27:7-14, Prov 20:22-23

6   Ezr 3:1-4:24, 1 Cor 2:6-3:4, Ps 28:1-9, Prov 20:24-25

7   Ezr 5:1-6:22, 1 Cor 3:5-23, Ps 29:1-11, Prov 20:26-27

8   Ezr 7:1-8:20, 1 Cor 4:1-21, Ps 30:1-12, Prov 20:28-30

9   Ezr 8:21-9:15, 1 Cor 5:1-13, Ps 31:1-8, Prov 21:1-2

10   Ezr 10:1-44, 1 Cor 6:1-20, Ps 31:9-18, Prov 21:3

11   Neh 1:1-3:14, 1 Cor 7:1-24, Ps 31:19-24, Prov 21:4

12   Neh 3:15-5:13, 1 Cor 7:25-40, Ps 32:1-11, Prov 21:5-7

13   Neh 5:14-7:60, 1 Cor 8:1-13, Ps 33:1-11, Prov 21:8-10

14   Neh 7:61-9:21, 1 Cor 9:1-18, Ps 33:12-22, Prov 21:11-12

15   Neh 9:22-10:39, 1 Cor 9:19-10:13, Ps 34:1-10, Prov 21:13

16   Neh 11:1-12:26, 1 Cor 10:14-11:2, Ps 34:11-22, Prov 21:14-16

208

AUGUST

17 Neh 12:27-13:31, 1 Cor 11:3-16, Ps 35:1-16, Prov 21:17-18

18 Est 1:1-3:15, 1 Cor 11:17-34, Ps 35:17-28, Prov 21:19-20

19 Est 4:1-7:10, 1 Cor 12:1-26, Ps 36:1-12, Prov 21:21-22

20 Est 8:1-10:3, 1 Cor 12:27-13:13, Ps 37:1-11, Prov 21:23-24

21 Job 1:1-3:26, 1 Cor 14:1-17, Ps 37:12-29, Prov 21:25-26

22 Job 4:1-7:21, 1 Cor 14:18-40, Ps 37:30-40, Prov 21:27

23 Job 8:1-11:20, 1 Cor 15:1-28, Ps 38:1-22, Prov 21:28-29

24 Job 12:1-15:35, 1 Cor 15:29-58, Ps 39:1-13, Prov 21:30-31

25 Job 16:1-19:29, 1 Cor 16:1-24, Ps 40:1-10, Prov 22:1

26 Job 20:1-22:30, 2 Cor 1:1-11, Ps 40:11-17, Prov 22:2-4

27 Job 23:1-27:23, 2 Cor 1:12-2:11, Ps 41:1-13, Prov 22:5-6

28 Job 28:1-30:31, 2 Cor 2:12-17, Ps 42:1-11, Prov 22:7

29 Job 31:1-33:33, 2 Cor 3:1-18, Ps 43:1-5, Prov 22:8-9

30 Job 34:1-36:33, 2 Cor 4:1-12, Ps 44:1-8, Prov 22:10-12

31 Job 37:1-39:30, 2 Cor 4:13-5:10, Ps 44:9-26, Prov 22:13

Confessing *God's Word*

1 Job 40:1-42:17, 2 Cor 5:11-21, Ps 45:1-17, Prov 22:14

2 Ecc 1:1-3:22, 2 Cor 6:1-13, Ps 46:1-11, Prov 22:15

3 Ecc 4:1-6:12, 2 Cor 6:14-7:7, Ps 47:1-9, Prov 22:16

4 Ecc 7:1-9:18, 2 Cor 7:8-16, Ps 48:1-14, Prov 22:17-19

5 Ecc 10:1-12:14, 2 Cor 8:1-15, Ps 49:1-20, Prov 22:20-21

6 Sng 1:1-4:16, 2 Cor 8:16-24, Ps 50:1-23, Prov 22:22-23

7 Sng 5:1-8:14, 2 Cor 9:1-15, Ps 51:1-19, Prov 22:24-25

8 Isa 1:1-2:22, 2 Cor 10:1-18, Ps 52:1-9, Prov 22:26-27

9 Isa 3:1-5:30, 2 Cor 11:1-15, Ps 53:1-6, Prov 22:28-29

10 Isa 6:1-7:25, 2 Cor 11:16-33, Ps 54:1-7, Prov 23:1-3

11 Isa 8:1-9:21, 2 Cor 12:1-10, Ps 55:1-23, Prov 23:4-5

12 Isa 10:1-11:16, 2 Cor 12:11-21, Ps 56:1-13, Prov 23:6-8

13 Isa 12:1-14:32, 2 Cor 13:1-14, Ps 57:1-11, Prov 23:9-11

14 Isa 15:1-18:7, Gal 1:1-24, Ps 58:1-11, Prov 23:12

15 Isa 19:1-21:17, Gal 2:1-16, Ps 59:1-17, Prov 23:13-14

16 Isa 22:1-24:23, Gal 2:17-3:9, Ps 60:1-12, Prov 23:15-16

September

17 Isa 25:1-28:13, Gal 3:10-22, PS 61:1-8, Prov 23:17-18

18 Isa 28:14-30:11, Gal 3:23-4:31, Ps 62:1-12, Prov 23:19-21

19 Isa 30:12-33:12, Gal 5:1-12, Ps 63:1-11, Prov 23:22

20 Isa 33:13-36:22, Gal 5:13-26, Ps 64:1-10, Prov 23:23

21 Isa 37:1-38:22, Gal 6:1-18, Ps 65:1-13, Prov 23:24-25

22 Isa 39:1-41:16, Eph 1:1-23, Ps 66:1-20, Prov 23:26-28

23 Isa 41:17-43:13, Eph 2:1-22, Ps 67:1-7, Prov 23:29-35

24 Isa 43:14-45:10, Eph 3:1-21, Ps 68:1-18, Prov 24:1-2

25 Isa 45:1-48:11, Eph 4:1-16, Ps 68:19-35, Prov 24:3-4

26 Isa 48:12-50:11, Eph 4:17-32, Ps 69:1-18, Prov 24:5-6

27 Isa 51:1-53:12, Eph 5:1-33, Ps 69:19-36, Prov 24:7

28 Isa 54:1-57:13, Eph 6:1-24, Ps 70:1-5, Prov 24:8

29 Isa 57:14-59:21, Php 1:1-26, Ps 71:1-24, Prov 24:9-10

30 Isa 60:1-62:5, Php 1:27-2:18, Ps 72:1-20, Prov 24:11-12

CONFESSING *God's Word*

1 Isa 62:6-65:25, Php 2:19-3:4a, Ps 73:1-28, Prov 24:13-14

2 Isa 66:1-24, Php 3:4b-21, Ps 74:1-23, Prov 24:15-16

3 Jer 1:1-2:30, Php 4:1-23, Ps 75:1-10, Prov 24:17-20

4 Jer 2:31-4:18, Col 1:1-20, Ps 76:1-12, Prov 24:21-22

5 Jer 4:19-6:14, Col 1:21-2:7, Ps 77:1-20, Prov 24:23-25

6 Jer 6:15-8:7, Col 2:8-23, Ps 78:1-31, Prov 24:26

7 Jer 8:8-9:26, Col 3:1-17, Ps 78:32-55, Prov 24:27

8 Jer 10:1-11:23, Col 3:18-4:18, Ps 78:56-72, Prov 24:28-29

9 Jer 12:1-14:10, 1 Th 1:1-2:9, Ps 79:1-13, Prov 24:30-34

10 Jer 14:11-16:15, 1 Th 2:10-3:13, Ps 80:1-19, Prov 25:1-5

11 Jer 16:16-18:23, 1 Th 4:1-5:3, Ps 81:1-16, Prov 25:6-7

12 Jer 19:1-21:14, 1 Th 5:4-28, Ps 82:1-8, Prov 25:8-10

13 Jer 22:1-23:20, 2 Th 1:1-12, Ps 83:1-18, Prov 25:11-14

14 Jer 23:21-25:38, 2 Th 2:1-17, Ps 84:1-12, Prov 25:15

15 Jer 26:1-27:22, 2 Th 3:1-18, Ps 85:1-13, Prov 25:16

16 Jer 28:1-29:32, 1 Tim 1:1-20, Ps 86:1-17, Prov 25:17

17 Jer 30:1-31:26, 1 Tim 2:1-15, Ps 87:1-7, Prov 25:18-19

18 Jer 31:27-32:44, 1 Tim 3:1-16, Ps 88:1-18, Prov 25:20-22

19 Jer 33:1-34:22, 1 Tim 4:1-16, Ps 89:1-13, Prov 25:23-24

20 Jer 35:1-36:32, 1 Tim 5:1-25, Ps 89:14-37, Prov 25:25-27

21 Jer 37:1-38:28, 1 Tim 6:1-21, Ps 89:38-52, Prov 25:28

22 Jer 39:1-41:18, 2 Tim 1:1-18, Ps 90:1-91:16, Prov 26:1-2

23 Jer 42:1-44:23, 2 Tim 2:1-21, Ps 92:1-93:5, Prov 26:3-5

24 Jer 44:24-47:7, 2 Tim 2:22-3:17, Ps 94:1-23, Prov 26:6-8

25 Jer 48:1-49:22, 2 Tim 4:1-22, Ps 95:1-96:13, Prov 26:9-12

26 Jer 49:23-50:26, Tit 1:1-16, Ps 97:1-98:9, Prov 26:13-16

27 Jer 51:1-53, Tit 2:1-15, Ps 99:1-9, Prov 26:17

28 Jer 51:54-52:34, Tit 3:1-15, Ps 100:1-5, Prov 26:18-19

29 Lam 1:1-2:19, Phm 1:1-25, Ps 101:1-8, Prov 26:20

30 Lam 2:20-3:66, Heb 1:1-14, Ps 102:1-28, Prov 26:21-22

31 Lam 4:1-5:22, Heb 2:1-18, Ps 103:1-22, Prov 26:23

CONFESSING *God's Word*

1 Ezk 1:1-3:15, Heb 3:1-19, Ps 104:1-23, Prov 26:24-26

2 Ezk 3:16-6:14, Heb 4:1-16, Ps 104:24-35, Prov 26:27

3 Ezk 7:1-9:11, Heb 5:1-14, Ps 105:1-15, Prov 26:28

4 Ezk 10:1-11:25, Heb 6:1-20, Ps 105:16-36, Prov 27:1-2

5 Ezk 12:1-14:11, Heb 7:1-17, Ps 105:37-45, Prov 27:3

6 Ezk 14:12-16:42, Heb 7:18-28, Ps 106:1-12, Prov 27:4-6

7 Ezk 16:43-17:24, Heb 8:1-13, Ps 106:13-31, Prov 27:7-9

8 Ezk 18:1-19:14, Heb 9:1-10, Ps 106:32-48, Prov 27:10

9 Ezk 20:1-49, Heb 9:11-28, Ps 107:1-43, Prov 27:11

10 Ezk 21:1-22:31, Heb 10:1-17, Ps 108:1-13, Prov 27:12

11 Ezk 23:1-49, Heb 10:18-39, Ps 109:1-31, Prov 27:13

12 Ezk 24:1-26:21, Heb 11:1-16, Ps 110:1-7, Prov 27:14

13 Ezk 27:1-28:26, Heb 11:17-31, Ps 111:1-10, Prov 27:15-16

14 Ezk 29:1-30:26, Heb 11:32-12:13, Ps 112:1-10, Prov 27:17

15 Ezk 31:1-32:32, Heb 12:14-29, Ps 113:1-114:8, Prov 27:18-20

16 Ezk 33:1-34:31, Heb 13:1-25, Ps 115:1-18, Prov 27:21-22

NOVEMBER

17 Ezk 35:1-36:38, Jm 1:1-18, Ps 116:1-19, Prov 27:23-27

18 Ezk 37:1-38:23, Jm 1:19-2:17, Ps 117:1-2, Prov 28:1

19 Ezk 39:1-40:27, Jm 2:18-3:18, Ps 118:1-18, Prov 28:2

20 Ezk 40:28-41:26, Jm 4:1-17, Ps 118:19-29, Prov 28:3-5

21 Ezk 42:1-43:27, Jm 5:1-20, Ps 119:1-16, Prov 28:6-7

22 Ezk 44:1-45:12, 1 Pet 1:1-12, Ps 119:17-32, Prov 28:8-10

23 Ezk 45:13-46:24, 1 Pet 1:13-2:10, Ps 119:33-48, Prov 28:11

24 Ezk 47:1-48:35, 1 Pet 2:11-3:7, Ps 119:49-64, Prov 28:12-13

25 Dan. 1:1-2:23, 1 Pet 3:8-4:6, Ps 119:65-80, Prov 28:14

26 Dan. 2:24-3:30, 1 Pet 4:7-5:14, Ps 119:81-96, Prov 28:15-16

27 Dan. 4:1-37, 2 Pet 1:1-21, Ps 119:97-112, Prov 28:17-18

28 Dan. 5:1-31, 2 Pet 2:1-22, Ps 119:113-128, Prov 28:19-20

29 Dan. 6:1-28, 2 Pet 3:1-18, Ps 119:129-152, Prov. 28:21-22

30 Dan 7:1-28, 1 Jn 1:1-10, Ps 119:153-176, Prov 28:23-24

CONFESSING *God's Word*

1 Dan 8:1-27, 1 Jn 2:1-17, Ps 120:1-7, Prov 28:25-26

2 Dan 9:1-11:1, 1 Jn 2:18-3:6, Ps 121:1-8, Prov 28:27-28

3 Dan 11:2-35, 1 Jn 3:7-24, Ps 122:1-9, Prov 29:1

4 Dan 11:36-12:13, 1 Jn 4:1-21, Ps 123:1-4 Prov 29:2-4

5 Hos 1:1-3:5, 1 Jn 5:1-21, Ps 124:1-8, Prov 29:5-8

6 Hos 4:1-5:15, 2 Jn 1:1-13, Ps 125:1-5, Prov 29:9-11

7 Hos 6:1-9:17, 3 Jn 1:1-14, Ps 126:1-6, Prov 29:12-14

8 Hos 10:1-14:9, Jude 1:1-25, Ps 127:1-5, Prov 29:15-17

9 Joel 1:1-3:21, Rev 1:1-20, Ps 128:1-6, Prov 29:18

10 Amos 1:1-3:15, Rev 2:1-17, Ps 129:1-8, Prov 29:19-20

11 Amos 4:1-6:14, Rev 2:18-3:6; Ps 130:1-8, Prov 29:21-22

12 Amos 7:1-9:15, Rev 3:7-22, Ps 131:1-3, Prov 29:23

13 Obad 1:1-21, Rev 4:1-11, Ps 132:1-18, Prov 29:24-25

14 Jonah 1:1-4:11, Rev 5:1-14, Ps 133:1-3, Prov 29:26-27

15 Mic 1:1-4:13, Rev 6:1-17, Ps 134:1-3, Prov 30:1-4

16 Mic 5:1-7:20, Rev 7:1-17, Ps 135:1-21, Prov 30:5-6

216

DECEMBER

17 Nah 1:1-3:19, Rev 8:1-13, Ps 136:1-26, Prov 30:7-9

18 Hab 1:1-3:19, Rev 9:1-21, Ps 137:1-9, Prov 30:10

19 Zeph 1:1-3:20, Rev 10:1-11, Ps 138:1-8, Prov 30:11-14

20 Hag 1:1-2:23, Rev 11:1-19, Ps 139:1-24, Prov 30:15-16

21 Zech 1:1-21, Rev 12:1-13:1a, Ps 140:1-13, Prov 30:17

22 Zech 2:1-3:10, Rev 13:1b-18, Ps 141:1-10, Prov 30:18-20

23 Zech 4:1-5:11, Rev 14:1-20, Ps 142:1-7, Prov 30:21-23

24 Zech 6:1-7:14, Rev 15:1-8, Ps 143:1-12, Prov 30:24-28

25 Zech 8:1-23, Rev, 16:1-21, Ps 144:1-15, Prov 30:29-31

26 Zech 9:1-17, Rev 17:1-18, Ps 145:1-21, Prov 30:32

27 Zech 10:1-11:17, Rev 18:1-24, Ps 146:1-10, Prov 30:33

28 Zech 12:1-13:9, Rev 19:1-21, Ps 147:1-20, Prov 31:1-7

29 Zech 14:1-21, Rev 20:1-15, Ps 148:1-14, Prov 31:8-9

30 Mal 1:1-2:17, Rev 21:1-27, Ps 149:1-9, Prov 31:10-24

31 Mal 3:1-4:6, Rev 22:1-21, Ps 150:1-6, Prov 31:25-31

CONFESSING *God's Word*

DR. MAUREEN ANDERSON

Resolved to leave an imprint for this generation and generations to come, Dr. Maureen Anderson has been teaching the Word of God since 1976. Counted among the most exciting and respected women in Christian ministry, her television programs are broadcast around the world. On one of Arizona's local secular stations, her television show has been ranked number one by Nielsen Ratings.

Dr. Maureen exhorts everyone who will listen to confess God's word each day, which expands your "love walk" with Jesus. A best-selling author and international speaker, Dr. Maureen writes from her own experiences and shares how God's love, grace, healing and prayer has led her to live an EXTRAORDINARY life. Her most recent book release is *A Marriage Beyond the Dream*. Among favorites are *Releasing the Miraculous Through Fasting with Prayer, Confessing God's Word, Damaged DNA, Toxic Emotions, Making Impossibilities Possible* and many others.

Dr. Maureen and her husband, Dr. Tom Anderson, are the Senior Pastors of The Living Word Bible Church located in Mesa, Arizona. Living Word Bible Church is considered to be one of the fastest growing churches in the nation with over nine thousand persons in attendance. Married for over forty years, she is the mother of two sons, Scot and Jason, who are in full-time ministry. She is also the grandmother of nine.

219

Salvation Prayer

Salvation does not mean following a bunch of rules to try and keep God happy. The truth is that He loves you and wants you to experience joy, health, peace and prosperity. You can only do that by knowing Jesus as a friend and savior.

How can you be saved? It is a matter of simply believing.

The Bible says:
If you confess with your mouth the Lord Jesus and believe in your heart that God has raised Him from the dead, you will be saved.
-Romans 10:9

If you believe, then pray this prayer:
"Dear Father God I ask you to forgive me of all of my sins. Jesus, come into my heart, come in to my life, be my Lord and Savior. In Jesus name, Amen. Jesus is Lord!"

Congratulations! You have made the very best decision you have ever made or ever will make. Now you are saved. You are forgiven and you are on your way to heaven. The next step is to grow in this new relationship with God. The best way to do that is to read your Bible every day so that God can speak to you through it and get involved in a good church so that you can have support and fellowship of other believers.

Now that you are saved, we would love to hear from you! Please call us at (480) 964-4463 so that we can come into agreement with you and bless you with a free Bible.

CONTACT US

To order products or for more information contact us at:

Living Word Bible Church
3520 East Brown Road
Mesa, Arizona 85213
Phone: (480) 964-4463

or visit our website at: livingwordonline.org.

TELEVISION BROADCASTS

Join the Anderson's television broadcasts which can be seen in the United States and around the world on stations such as, TBN, Day Star, Fox, TCC, UPN, AZTV and WBUW. Check your local listings for times and stations in your area.